JEFF FLYGARE

Close Reading in the Secondary Classroom

MARZANO
— Research —

THE CLASSROOM STRATEGIES SERIES

555 North Morton Street
Bloomington, IN 47404
888.849.0851
FAX: 866.801.1477

email: info@MarzanoResearch.com
MarzanoResearch.com

Visit **marzanoresearch.com/classroomstrategies** to download the free reproducibles in this book.

Printed in the United States of America

Library of Congress Control Number: 2017915169

ISBN: 978-1-943360-01-7

22 21 20 19 18   1 2 3 4 5

Text and Cover Designer: Abigail Bowen

MARZANO RESEARCH DEVELOPMENT TEAM

Director of Content & Resources
Julia A. Simms

Editorial Manager
Laurel Hecker

Proficiency Scale Analyst
Christopher Dodson

Editorial Assistant / Staff Writer
Jacob Wipf

Marzano Research Associates

Mario Acosta	Jason E. Harlacher	Kristin Poage
Tina H. Boogren	Tammy Heflebower	Cameron Rains
Toby Boss	Lynne Herr	Tom Roy
Robin J. Carey	Mitzi Hoback	Mike Ruyle
Bev Clemens	Jan K. Hoegh	Roberta Selleck
Douglas Finn III	Jeanie Iberlin	Julia A. Simms
Michelle Finn	Bettina Kates	Gerry Varty
Jane Doty Fischer	Jessica McIntyre	Phil Warrick
Jeff Flygare	Rebecca Mestaz	David C. Yanoski
Laura Hack	Diane E. Paynter	Bill Zima

ACKNOWLEDGMENTS

Marzano Research would like to thank the following reviewers:

Sharon Borton
Vice Principal
Victory Middle School
Meridian, Idaho

Debbie Duffee
English Teacher
Hallsville High School
Hallsville, Texas

Julie Ray
Reading Teacher
Taylor Road Middle School
Johns Creek, Georgia

Visit **marzanoresearch.com/classroomstrategies**
to download the free reproducibles in this book.

CONTENTS

Reproducibles are in italics.

CHAPTER 3

READING TWICE AND ANNOTATING 41

CHAPTER 4

GENERATING QUESTIONS AND READING ANALYTICALLY 63

CHAPTER 5

DISCUSSING AS A CLASS OR ANALYZING INDIVIDUALLY, AND USING PROCESSING ACTIVITIES 75

CHAPTER 6

PLANNING AND ASSESSING CLOSE READING 87

ABOUT THE AUTHOR

Jeff Flygare is a former classroom teacher, English department chair, professional developer, and building-level leader. During his twenty-six-year career teaching high school English, he taught nearly every course in the department. Jeff developed classes in mythology, Shakespeare, philosophy, and comparative religions, and worked with social studies colleagues to create an interdisciplinary class called world studies, which he team-taught successfully for seventeen years. He taught advanced placement (AP) English classes for twenty-one years and served as an AP English literature reader and table leader for Educational Testing Service for many years.

Jeff also has a strong theatrical background, working first as an actor and then as a director at a major regional theater company in Colorado. He directed many high school productions, both traditional and Shakespearean. As a Marzano Research associate, Jeff travels around the United States and across the world to work with educators on topics involving curriculum, instruction, and assessment.

He holds a bachelor's degree in English from the State University of New York at Buffalo, a master's degree in English from the University of Colorado Denver, and a master's degree in education with an endorsement in gifted education from the University of Colorado Colorado Springs.

ABOUT MARZANO RESEARCH

Marzano Research is a joint venture between Solution Tree and Dr. Robert J. Marzano. Marzano Research combines Dr. Marzano's fifty years of educational research with continuous action research in all major areas of schooling in order to provide effective and accessible instructional strategies, leadership strategies, and classroom assessment strategies that are always at the forefront of best practice. By providing such an all-inclusive research-into-practice resource center, Marzano Research provides teachers and principals with the tools they need to effect profound and immediate improvement in student achievement.

INTRODUCTION

Close Reading in the Secondary Classroom is part of a series of books collectively referred to as *The Classroom Strategies Series*. This series aims to provide teachers, as well as building and district administrators, with an in-depth treatment of research-based instructional strategies that can be used in the classroom to enhance student achievement. Many of the strategies addressed in this series have been covered in other works, such as *Classroom Instruction That Works* (Marzano, Pickering, & Pollock, 2001), *Classroom Management That Works* (Marzano, 2003), *The New Art and Science of Teaching* (Marzano, 2017), and *Effective Supervision* (Marzano, Frontier, & Livingston, 2011). Although those works devoted a chapter or part of a chapter to particular strategies, *The Classroom Strategies Series* devotes an entire book to an instructional strategy or set of related strategies.

The purpose of this book is to provide a method and associated strategies to secondary classroom teachers for introducing and developing students' skill of close reading. Today, with the emphasis on the Common Core State Standards (CCSS), as well as individual state standards on literacy and critical thinking, close reading has become a vital skill for all secondary students (whether or not they pursue postsecondary education). Further, close reading is a skill that applies far beyond the English language arts classroom. Thus, *Close Reading in the Secondary Classroom* is aimed at a wide range of secondary teachers, not only those who teach traditional reading curricula. The strategies suggested here are useful in the mathematics and physical education classrooms just as much as they are in an English language arts or social studies classroom.

Close Reading in the Secondary Classroom begins with a discussion of why close reading is a vital skill to secondary students. The first chapter defines close reading, describes its importance, and discusses the history of literary criticism. The specific steps of the close reading process are listed at the end of the chapter.

The six steps of this process include:

1. Prereading (covered in chapter 2)

2. Reading twice and annotating (covered in chapter 3)

3. Generating questions (covered in chapter 4)

4. Reading analytically (covered in chapter 4)

5. Discussing as a class or analyzing individually (covered in chapter 5)

6. Using processing activities (covered in chapter 5)

Please note that chapters 4 and 5 each cover two steps. Chapters 2 through 5 present a thorough discussion of each step in the close reading process, with instructional strategies and suggestions for implementing each step in the classroom. On the whole, this process provides students with a structure for understanding and mastering close reading of challenging texts. Chapter 6 briefly examines the issues around planning for and assessment of close reading with secondary students. Because close reading is a robust and complicated skill that will be used in most classrooms throughout the entire school year, teachers need to consider special issues when planning instruction and assessment.

Definition of Close Reading

For some people, *close reading* means re-encountering the text many times, gaining insights through the response of the reader to new elements in the text with each additional reading. For others, close reading is the act of focusing on a selection of text with a particular lens, looking at what the text has to offer when one looks for something specific.

In this book, close reading is a way to drill down into a selected text and approach what an author is doing on a deep level. An easy way to further define close reading is to see the activity as an attempt to deeply understand a text by looking at the author's choices and their effects. As noted in this resource, students need to focus on the formalist elements of the text for creating meaning. Once they have identified meaning through these methods, they may find enhanced importance to their own reaction to the text. We live in a world of accountability in public education, and that accountability sometimes comes in the form of standardized tests. In a test situation, it is especially important for the student to be able to analyze the text in a manner that arrives at a commonly accepted meaning—one that can be a correct answer to a test item. Forms of analysis based outside the text are too subjective. One cannot know a great deal about the author's intentions, and one can often know too much about the reader's reactions. When a reader first encounters a text, he or she often ponders what is happening. In other words, the reader first wants to understand plot, literal meaning, and other surface-level concerns. Beyond that, the reader might wonder what the author is doing in the text. Such analysis is deeper than asking what is happening because it looks to the effect a text has on the reader. A text may create an emotional response in the reader, it may emphasize a point, or an author may attempt to manipulate the reader's response in some way. These, and potentially an infinite number of additional responses, may legitimately answer the question of what the author is doing.

When an author creates an effect, identifying it is relatively pointless if the reader doesn't go on to ask the obvious follow-up questions of "Why?" and "How?" Depending on the text, these questions can take many forms, such as the following examples.

- Why would an author choose to develop a feeling of sadness?

- What is the effect of the author's emerging purpose in the passage?

- Further, how is the author creating that feeling of _____?

- What word choice is the author employing?

- What imagery, symbols, syntax, and point of view is the author using?

- What is the specific effect of each choice on the reader, and what is the cumulative effect of the choices on the passage?

Once a student can accurately answer questions like these, he or she can be said to be close reading a passage.

Close reading allows the reader to participate with the author in his or her project, not simply as a receiver but as a thinking, feeling, responding, and intelligent human being. This has value for the reader. Students will begin to understand the power of the written word, the way the author's agenda affects their world, and they will develop the ability to respond thoughtfully to an author's ideas. If one of the purposes of K–12 education is to develop well-informed, reasoning, thoughtful citizens, close reading is an essential skill (Student Achievement Partners, 2016).

Let's be clear about what close reading is *not*. Close reading is not a series of reader responses loosely tied to a text. The meaning the reader generates may or may not be valid. Validity emerges out of a close examination of a text in light of a reader's response. If the text—through careful, accurate analysis—supports that response, then the reader's response is valid and meaningful.

Close reading offers the analytical tools and the common nomenclature that can start a discussion about meaning. It is a technique with universal content-area application, but it takes years to develop in students. The aim of this book is to offer the methods and teaching suggestions that will allow students to gain this valuable skill, a skill that will serve them beyond their secondary education.

How to Use This Book

Educators can use *Close Reading in the Secondary Classroom* as a self-study text that provides an in-depth understanding of close reading as a process and an instructional strategy. Each chapter provides useful instructional strategies or ideas related to developing the ability of students to effectively close read. As you progress through the chapters, you will also find comprehension questions at the end of chapters 2 through 6. It is important to complete these questions and compare your answers with those in appendix A (page 101). Such interaction provides a review of the content and allows a thorough examination of your understanding. Groups or teams of teachers who wish to examine close reading in their classrooms may also use *Close Reading in the Secondary Classroom*. Team members should answer the questions independently and then compare their answers in small- or large-group settings. Appendix B (page 107) includes three examples of close reading: two literary and one informational. The examples observe a classroom and the teacher's real-time interactions with students.

Chapter 1

RESEARCH AND THEORY

In this chapter, we start with why close reading is a very important skill for every secondary school student and describe one method for practicing close reading in the secondary classroom. As background for understanding the importance of close reading, we will also look briefly at the history of literary criticism—the foundational methodology behind modern close reading processes for secondary students. Then, to further define close reading for the purposes of this book, we'll review some research applicable to the strategy of close reading. We'll discuss the importance of two factors in considering close reading in the classroom: (1) research background and (2) instructional shifts. Finally, we'll close on the steps of the close reading process.

The Need for Close Reading

Today, the written word conflicts not just with movies and television but also with digital texts that are lively and interactive, value action over thought, and provide a level of engagement with which the lightly encountered written word cannot compete. The written word demands more than a simple reading of the story; it demands work—questioning the text and interacting at an intellectual level that movies and video games often do not require. We could examine the value our culture places on such action-based encounters and the rejection—though perhaps not consciously—of intellectual life, but to what end? American culture is what it is, and it isn't likely to change soon. In a culture that tends to preach activity over thought, sports over the arts, and the politics of action over the politics of contemplation, students may be unlikely to choose an evening with a good book over an evening with the latest video game.

Yet we live in a globally connected world, and students will grow up to compete for jobs with global citizens from very different cultures, many of which value great ideas, great minds, and the role of a thinking and reasoning human engaged with the world. As such, we as teachers have a responsibility to value critical thinking, model it for students, and ask students to make every attempt to fully actualize the brains they have.

Most educators are aware that the skill of reading well is essential for success in school, the working world, and life. But it may well be that we never examine the underlying question: Why? There are pedantic answers to that question—to be informed, to share information, to understand job responsibilities, and so on. But to go beyond these mundane responses we must ask the question, "Why should we read?" Susan Wise Bauer (2003), in her book *The Well-Educated Mind*, begins her chapter on the art of reading with the claim that most futurists believe and have declared:

> We are a postliterate culture. Books are outdated forms of communication. Soon the flood of information that is now contained in books, magazines, and newspapers will be sorted by artificial intelligence and presented in multimedia formats. No more boring print. (p. 24)

Bauer (2003) goes on to explain that there is still a role for print in the world, but changes since the publication of her book suggest the futurists' vision of the new nonprint world may be closer than she imagined. Anyone who has spent more than a few weeks in a 21st century secondary school classroom will agree that students today don't read as much as those of prior generations.

Why should we read? When we return to that question, the real answer has less to do with pragmatic necessity in our now primarily digital lives and more to do with what reading print material does *to* us. The act of reading the printed word (more than just reading the words for surface meaning) is the process of taking words and unpacking their ideas and deeper meanings. Reading is an intentional action that helps create and influence our view of ourselves as thinking beings with values that are cultural, social, and even political and theological.

In a world of digital interactivity, students grow up expecting to engage with every experience by allowing the experience to engage them. This is fundamentally passive. Interactive video games and other digital media do the work of engaging users. Books, on the other hand, require readers to do the work, using their intellect and imagination to fully experience the text. When students are accustomed to digital media, they may bring those expectations to printed texts, and their reading experiences suffer as a result.

For some educators, the conventional wisdom is to adjust their instruction to meet students' expectations of passive engagement. However, this does students a disservice. At some point, students need to experience the joy of actively engaging in a great essay or novel. At some point, they need to be able to read more than the story, more than the words on the page, more than for the simple quiz on the chapter. They need to bring themselves to the text. As one of my graduate professors often said, "Your reading of a text is only as good as the questions you ask. And if you ask no questions of the text, it will yield no answers" (B. Mudge, personal communication, September 5, 1997). Students need to know what questions to ask and how to answer them.

The standards movement has precipitated a stronger emphasis on the ability to read, analyze, and report on challenging texts, both literary and informational (Student Achievement Partners, 2016). As the standards movement developed, the emphasis on informational text developed with it (Kendall, 2011). English language arts teachers found themselves in a position of having to add the study of informational texts more often into their curricula. Social studies teachers had taught informational texts for years, but they found an increased emphasis on the analysis of primary sources, which often challenge students with difficult ideas and unfamiliar styles.

Standards in English language arts (and to a lesser extent in social studies) often depict a sharp division between literary and informational texts. A closer examination, however, reveals an enormous degree of overlap in the skills needed to address these two kinds of texts. Consider these two eighth-grade Common Core Reading standards, one for informational texts and one for literary texts:

> RI.8.2: Determine a central idea of a text and analyze its development over the course of the text, including its relationship to supporting ideas; provide an objective summary of the text. (National Governors Association Center for Best Practices & Council of Chief State School Officers [NGA & CCSSO], 2010)

> RL.8.2: Determine a theme or central idea of a text and analyze its development over the course of the text, including its relationship to the characters, setting, and plot; provide an objective summary of the text. (NGA & CCSSO, 2010)

While a few terms differ, these two standards represent the same skill set. We might wonder why there are multiple separate standards that address the same skills. One answer is that the authors of these standards wanted to send a strong message about the importance of teaching the analysis of informational text, a genre that has traditionally held a lesser place in the English language arts curriculum (Kendall, 2011). In making this judgment, the creators of the state standards were correct. The ability to understand and analyze informational text is a basic skill every student must master. Students who go on to higher education will clearly spend the majority of their reading on informational texts, and if one considers the reading one does in daily life, be it for leisure or career, most is informational text. It is a basic life skill.

Secondary teachers of English, social studies, and the wide range of content areas that access state or Common Core English language arts standards must develop students' abilities to read critically and analyze an informational or literary text. These standards are challenging, and teachers face the limitations of time and student interest as they accept this challenge. It may well be that teachers sometimes choose to provide teacher-led analysis of a text as a method of saving time in a crowded curriculum. After all, they may reason, teacher-led analysis is better than no analysis at all. While that may be true, it does not lead students to develop their abilities to read and analyze a text *independently*, as required by the standards. That means we must adjust how we lead students to texts and focus on the gradual increase of their abilities to connect with a challenging text and unpack the author's meaning and method. One way of accomplishing this is through the art of close reading. Close reading is a skill that students develop over many years, with many teachers in many classrooms. It provides students a way to engage with a text, think deeply about it, and form well-supported opinions about it. In developing a deeper understanding of close reading, we should consider how it emerged as an analytical strategy.

The History of Close Reading

Close analysis of text is the result of centuries of emerging literary analysis (Richter, 2007). People have not always read intentionally and analytically, but from the earliest days, analysts have sought methods to understand texts in deep ways and go beyond the words on the page for both literary and informational texts (Richter, 2007). The various schools of literary criticism are the result of centuries of careful development and represent a wide range of methods to approach a text analytically. Thus, an important starting point for understanding the close reading process is examining the development of these literary-critical schools.

The first person to write about the interpretation of human writing was Plato (Richter, 1998). Actually, it is likely he wasn't the first, but his is the first writing to survive to the present day. Plato presents his ideas through a historical character, Socrates, about whom we know very little beyond what Plato includes in his dialogues. Plato (380 BCE/1992) gives short shrift to poets in *The Republic*, the book-length dialogue describing Socrates's vision of the ideal society. Socrates banishes the poets from his city-state, claiming they cannot be trusted to transmit the proper values to young people, thus indicating that the written word does more than just relate a story. Even within the decisions the Greek hero Achilles made in Homer's *Iliad*, Socrates interprets a value system that promotes self-interest over the good of the many, something he would not have influencing the young audience of Homer's epic. Though Socrates is a harsh critic, his comments indicate he sees the power of written language to influence the young.

Some decades after Plato described Socrates's views, Aristotle (335 BCE/1997) took a different position on written language. Aristotle's perspective on art is *mimetic*—it imitates nature. The more similar the art is to its object of imitation, the higher its quality. In his *Poetics*, which modern scholars believe is little more than a collection of his lecture notes, Aristotle described the *tragedy*, the form of drama the Athenians so perfected in the 4th century BCE. Unlike Plato, Aristotle was less interested in the influence a writer might have over the reader (or in the case of tragedy, the audience) and much more interested in how a playwright accomplishes the effects he creates on the stage (Richter, 1998). In this, Aristotle might be considered the first close reader, aiming at a solid analysis of what the writer is doing in the text. Aristotle introduced the concepts of *catharsis*, the release of the emotions of pity and fear that occurs, in Aristotle's opinion, most effectively when timed at the crisis of the play; *peripeteia*, an unexpected turn of events; and *anagnorisis*, the protagonist's discovery of new knowledge. Aristotle analyzed Sophocles's play *Oedipus Tyrannus* as an example of the best of Greek tragedy. In focusing on an example he considered the height of the genre, Aristotle (335 BCE/1997) described what the perfect tragedy ought to do and thus moved criticism from an analytical to a prescriptive perspective.

Such a structural view of the function of tragedy represents the first unpacking of a creative text known in Western literature and thus serves as the beginning of literary criticism. In taking such an analytical approach, Aristotle suggested that many texts hide more substantial interpretations beneath seemingly innocuous statements and events. By properly approaching a text, you can unpack these interpretations and thus see more than a surface reading of the text. Of course, such an approach does suggest questions about limits and extents: How many interpretations should there be? Are all interpretations valid? Does every text yield multiple interpretations, or even one additional interpretation, beyond the narrative story? When should you stop analyzing? Literary critics struggle with these issues to this very day, and as teachers share close reading and the interpretation of written text with their students, they will struggle with many of the same questions.

Following Aristotle, little substantial change in interpretive reading of texts occurred until the 19th century. It was not until the emergence of the modern era, with a wider range of philosophical and scientific approaches to understanding the world, that new approaches to literary criticism emerged, including formalism, Marxist criticism, feminist criticism, reader-response criticism, and deconstructionism. These important critical approaches provide different "lenses" through which a text may be interpreted. While we wish our students to approach texts from the lens of formalism, each of these approaches has had an important impact on our interpretation of literary texts, and students may use one or more of these approaches in their own personal reaction to a text, so a familiarity with each is important to teachers as they guide student analysis of texts.

Modern Criticism

Political, philosophical, and theological concerns supplanted much new thinking in the West until the Renaissance. Although there were literary critics and writers, such as Dante, Sir Philip Sidney, John Dryden, and Alexander Pope, who added to the literature interpretation discussion, there were no enormous revisions in the way people read and interpreted texts until the emergence of many schools of literary criticism in the 19th century (Richter, 1998).

During the 18th and early 19th centuries, critics were mainly concerned with whether texts conformed to classical models and often viewed the value of texts by the degree to which they conformed or didn't (Richter, 1998). Classical models were something to be admired and seen as a route to some underlying truth behind culture, a truth tied to an adoration of a lost ideal in the classical world. Scholars developed a key idea during this period: that the reading of important literary works would improve one's ethical standing. George Eliot (1856) perhaps most elegantly stated this in her essay

"The Natural History of German Life." Reading good books made you a better person. As of the early 20th century, scholars were still justifying the teaching of literature that way, and, indeed, the entry of literary study into public schools was grounded in this idea.

Organized systems of interpreting literature emerged as literature made its way into colleges and secondary schools. These schools of literary criticism each focused on a set of agreed-on philosophical presuppositions that affected, to a large extent, the interpretation that resulted. Initially, there were two important schools of literary criticism: (1) biographical and (2) historical.

Biographical criticism has been around since at least the 18th century, and Samuel Johnson (1779–1781) used it in his important work *The Lives of the Most Eminent English Poets*, which was enormously popular right into the 20th century. Biographical criticism is intuitively attractive, particularly to those who place great authors on high pedestals. It suggests that, as every reader suspects, much of what happens in the author's life impacts his or her writing. Thus, *biographical criticism* strove to analyze the biographies of writers and find connections to their works to read those works more deeply.

For example, biographical critics would point to profound moments in the life of American novelist Edith Wharton that arguably influenced events in her novel *Ethan Frome* (1911/1992). Wharton, who grew up in 19th century New York City, was raised in a family that shared all the Victorian taboos about women's sexual feelings. Taught to ignore emerging desires as an adolescent, her emotions escaped in a frequent and terrifying anxiety every time she returned to her parents' house. Her fear and anxiety were often so profound she was unable to walk inside the house and had to wait at the threshold for the symptoms to pass (Wharton, 1911/1992). Knowing that episode of Wharton's biography can be telling when reading *Ethan Frome*. This novel describes a Massachusetts farmer, a former engineering student, who finds himself locked in a loveless marriage and a career he adopted out of necessity rather than interest. Into this barren life comes his wife's beautiful cousin Mattie Silver. Ethan resists his growing desire for the beautiful girl but cannot deny it. Throughout the novel, the reader is placed in the position of observing important events from beyond a threshold, often a closed door beyond which things are clearly occurring (but which the reader is not privy to). Perhaps more important is the thematic implication of the threshold, where Ethan wishes to express his desire for Mattie but repeatedly stops before doing so—on the threshold of action, so to speak.

While a biographical reading like this may be correct and inform our understanding of the novel, it is certainly not the only way to read *Ethan Frome*. One of the limitations of biographical criticism is the way it implies that nonbiographical interpretations of a text are somehow less valid than biographical ones. Further, biographical criticism has an inherent flaw: one must know the author's biography. The fact is, the biographies of the vast majority of writers are unknown. Even in the case of William Shakespeare, regarded as the greatest playwright in the English language, words like *may*, *might*, and *could* signal the uncertainty and speculation of his biographies. The facts known about Shakespeare are few, and the documents from his life even fewer. Sparse data limit the biographical criticism available on our most important writers. Indeed, biographical criticism would have nothing at all to say about the most prolific author in the English language—anonymous.

Simultaneously with biographical criticism, literary critics also favored a historical view of the analysis of written texts. The basic presupposition of *historical criticism* is that understanding the historical moment of the text creation—particularly the political, theological, cultural, and social contexts—provides insights into interpretive meanings of texts (Historical criticism, 2014). While history is more readily accessible than an author's biography, fundamental flaws also exist in this approach to interpreting texts. First, not all historical periods are equally knowable. We know a great deal more, for example, about the French Revolution in the late 18th century than we do about the historical events surrounding the Trojan War. Indeed, some are not even sure the Trojan War was a real historical event. Also, while history is more knowable, the question arises as to *whose history* is the accepted version. There is an adage that history is written by the winners. There is truth to this, and history students will report that any important historical event viewed from the perspective of the losers looks very different from the commonly accepted version. Further, historical criticism starts from the assumption of the strong effect of the historical moment on the author as he or she composes a text. But surely there have been authors who have not succumbed to that influence or who have, like the French philosopher Montaigne, withdrawn from their own society. There are important examples of this throughout the history of literature; in these cases, the historical critic is unsure how to proceed. Historical criticism, while an important step forward beyond the biographical, was clearly not the answer for literary critics.

Formalism

As literary criticism moved into the 20th century, critics sought to bring a more stringent analysis, one grounded in the intrinsic elements of the text (Richter, 1998)—in other words, those portions of the text that can be identified and analyzed separately, using agreed-on analytical techniques. The result of this effort was what has come to be known as *formalism*. Formalism sought a scientific approach to interpretation of the written word. At its heart was a fundamental shift in the way critical reading was applied to the written text. Rather than seeing the text as an author's product or a historical moment, early formalism sought to see the text as an object in and of itself, independent of the influence of anything else. Early American formalists advocated seeing the text as a microcosm—a totally self-referential text world (Richter, 1998). The critical reader approached the text analytically to view that world. To do this, formalism accepts some of the precepts of the scientific method and applies them to the analysis of the written word. Science approaches the understanding of a phenomenon by isolating the object of study and applying a universally agreed-on, carefully defined, repeatable scientific method to its analysis. In applying this to literature, formalists began by isolating the subject of their analysis, the text. They claimed that the influence of an author on his or her writing was not to be considered in interpreting the text. Further, the reader's reaction, which can vary widely, could not be considered either. If one was to approach a written text scientifically, then the written text on the page must be the sole object of scrutiny (Richter, 1998).

Next, formalists needed a set of analytical tools to apply to the written text. Eventually, these tools became the well-known set of literary strategies still taught in English classes today—the *elements of literature*. These include plot structure, characterization, point of view, figurative language, tone, and theme, to name a few. In attempting to emulate the repeatability of scientific analysis, formalists advocated a very specific method of analyzing these elements. They claimed that if literary critics all studied the same text and properly analyzed that text through the elements of literature, each critic would arrive independently at the same, single, correct interpretation (Richter, 1998).

In the 21st century, few people would wholly agree with this approach to interpreting texts. Most people have been taught that the influence of the reader in unpacking meaning is as valuable and important as the text itself. Some argue that the author's intention should also be taken into consideration when interpreting a text (Richter, 1998). Yet formalism had a long run and found advocates well into the 20th century. The idea of one right answer continues to be appealing, especially for situations such as standardized test questions on the interpretation of a passage.

Although formalism as a school of criticism has lost its rank as the primary method of interpretation, it still has a place in the wider world of literary criticism today. Formalism provided other critical theories with the nomenclature and tools of analysis those theories use. Thus, when a reader-response critic (see page 13) or feminist critic (see page 12) discusses a passage, he or she will speak about theme, tone, or figurative language. In addition, formalism still provides students with the analytical tools they need to read and interpret written texts.

While literary critics' primary interpretive method was formalism, by the middle of the 20th century, things had begun to change (Crews, n.d.). A series of interpretive methods that brought other points of view to the reading and interpreting of texts began to emerge. Many of the critical schools rejected the formalist notion that a text is a thing in isolation (Richter, 1998). These methods include Marxist, feminist, and deconstructionist theories. Most of these schools viewed a written text as a product, not just of an author, but also of a culture that strongly influenced the creation of the text, which might adhere to cultural norms or reject them (Richter, 1998). One way to think about these methods is to consider them as *lenses* one applies when reading and interpreting texts. Each lens will clarify a particular perspective on the passage in question. In approaching the interpretation of texts from a variety of viewpoints, these methods signal a moment when regularity and agreement on meaning were less valued than before, reflecting the shift in Western cultural values more broadly (Crews, n.d.). At this point, many literary critics also began to look for diversity of perspectives, not just in their criticism, but also in the texts themselves, and pushed back against the notion of the *Western canon*, which predominantly consisted of dead, white, male, Judeo-Christian, straight writers (Richter, 1998).

Marxist Criticism

The ideas of Karl Marx and Friedrich Engels—particularly of the struggle between socioeconomic classes of the proletariat (workers) and bourgeoisie (owners of the means of production)—have had an enormous effect on the study of history, politics, and economics (Magee, 2001; Popkin, 2000). Literary critics have not missed the opportunity to apply the Marxist notion of economics and social structure to literature, providing a lens that can be productive in interpretation (Richter, 1998). Foundational to a Marxist approach to literature is the idea that history is economic. From a Marxist perspective, history can be reinterpreted not as a series of actions by great men (kings, generals, politicians) or great countries but as the working out of class struggles, with economics driving historical decisions. Marx owed a great deal to philosopher Georg Hegel, who saw the world in terms of conflict, with opposing powers constantly in a struggle to allow a world spirit to reveal and fulfill itself (Magee, 2001). Marx saw the struggle as primarily one of class. He also advocated using history as a political weapon in promoting the emergence and triumph of the proletariat in its struggle against the bourgeoisie (Magee, 2001). Marxist literary critics are often unafraid of taking Marx's advice in this matter and reread literature as a weapon against Western capitalism.

Critic Warren Montag (1992) provided one example of how the Marxist lens can yield a very different reading of a text. In his article "The 'Workshop of Filthy Creation': A Marxist Reading of *Frankenstein*," Montag (1992) rewrote the traditional reading of Mary W. Shelley's (1818/1992) famous novel. Readers often interpret *Frankenstein* as a comment on the limitations of science, suggesting there are actions that scientists—even if they could—should not take. Death is meant to be final, and the reanimation of dead flesh means that a scientist at some point is playing God. Readers often take the ending of the novel, tragic for both creation and creator, to mean that some things are better left unknown.

Montag (1992), on the other hand, approached the novel from the perspective of class. Victor Frankenstein, brought up in a wealthy home, provided with a first-class education, and clearly a part of the ruling class, is the perfect example of the bourgeoisie. In animating his creature, he is in fact, through his horrible actions, giving birth to a symbol of proletariat man. In the conflict between these two characters, Shelley captured the fundamental conflict of *Western capitalism*—the need of the bourgeoisie to create, use, and control the proletariat, and the desire of the proletariat to rise beyond that control and be totally independent. This is a very different reading of the novel, but a legitimate one nevertheless.

Placing the presuppositions of Marxist criticism on the reading of any text, particularly a nonfiction one, can help students quickly see the results of changes in perspective and help them understand that different readers can experience the same text very differently.

Feminist Criticism

Equally surprising are the changes that emerge when looking at a work through a feminist lens. As feminism became more and more a force in Western culture through the mid and late 20th century, literary critics sought to apply some of the basic presuppositions of feminism to the interpretation of literature (Richter, 2007). There are many feminisms, approaches all sharing the basic ideas of feminism but approaching literary interpretation with different agendas (Richter, 1998). Still, there are a few common traits nearly all feminisms share, and they are often focused on the politics of gender.

First, feminism focuses on the fact that men designed and benefit from patriarchy, a system of government, culture, and civilization. Although it may appear to be normal, patriarchy is not inherent or natural to human society. Patriarchy only appears normal because it has been in operation for so long and because men have kept themselves in decision-making positions that allow them to perpetuate the system. An important effect of patriarchy is that it robs women of their identity through objectification. Because patriarchy encourages males to act on their propensity to see women as objects of sexual desire, it places women only in that role, and therefore removes the possibility of women having identities beyond that objectification. Therefore, patriarchy is the problem, and feminism seeks to overturn it as a system (Richter, 1998).

In applying these ideas to literature, approaching a traditional story by focusing on gender and the problems of patriarchy will yield yet another (and quite legitimate) reading. As feminist critics examined the Western canon, they criticized the fact that male authors wrote a disproportionate number of these works (Richter, 1997; Woolf & Gordon, 2005). Some women-authored works relegated to secondary status (or worse) at the time of their publication were rediscovered as feminism gained acceptance. One such work is Kate Chopin's novella *The Awakening*, written in 1899, which literary critics virtually ignored until the middle of the 20th century. Today, *The Awakening* is one of the most studied texts in college classrooms and some high schools (Chopin, 1899/1994), but it took a shift in the way society views gender roles and the objectification of women for that change to occur.

Applying a feminist perspective to major events and character interactions in a text can yield some fascinating authorial moves that a formalist reading might not.

Postmodernism

The ideas of *postmodernism* (for example, skepticism, the rejection of objective truth, knowledge as socially constructed, and so on) also found their way into the interpretation of writing in the late 1960s and the years following. One example of this is *poststructuralism*. Poststructuralist critics desired to remove the structures traditional culture had placed on the reader's view of the written text. A traditional view focuses on binaries—good versus evil, black versus white, United States versus the world, and a whole variety of dichotomous approaches to understanding ideas. Poststructuralism sought to identify the complexities of the world, to show that difficult ideas resist the reduction to simplistic two-sided discussions. While there is an appeal in identifying the complexities of human life and applying this to the reading of a text, poststructuralism was also seen as an attack on a more traditional or conservative worldview.

Perhaps the deepest and most challenging form of poststructuralism is deconstructionism. Emerging out of language theory, *deconstructionism* identified the disconnect that can occur between the written word on the page and the thing it refers to—between the signifier and the signified (Richter, 1998). Deconstructionists point out that writing itself perpetuates the distance between signifier and signified because the gap between the two continually grows as language proceeds. Eventually, meaning itself is lost in this disconnect. Starting there, deconstructionists sought to reject nearly all Western culture traditions and began an attack on the Western canon. If language defers meaning, meaning cannot be the source of our understanding of the value of a text. If that is true, no one text is better than any other. A text by an author outside the Western tradition is no better than a traditional canonical text. Once at this philosophical point, one can attack the very idea of a text. Soon, one can read nearly everything with meaning, connotation, theme, and purpose (Richter, 1998). While deconstructionism does not play a significant role in close reading as this book describes, it is an important critical lens and an interesting look into how far literary theory can go.

Reader-Response Criticism

Another important approach to interpreting literature is *reader-response criticism*. While the role of the reader in experiencing literature had been sidelined during various historical periods (for example, during the Romantic period of the late 18th and early 19th centuries, which prioritized the "genius" of the artist), by the 20th century, literary critics were re-establishing the vital role of the reader or audience in experiencing literature (Richter, 1998). One way to understand reader-response theory is to see it as something like the opposite of formalism. Formalism identifies the text as the sole object of scrutiny—the roles of the author and the reader are not important to the creation of meaning. Reader-response theory examines the reaction of the reader as the key element in establishing meaning. Wayne C. Booth (1961) expressed this idea most fully in *The Rhetoric of Fiction*.

One inherent difficulty with the reader-response method is its potential to generate as many readings of a text as there are readers of the text. While it is correct that the reader is vital to the creation of textual meaning, students practicing close reading will need to share a common method that produces common results. Further, the common elements of literary criticism provide the basis for standardized tests, not the response of the reader. Although reader-response theory has its role in the interpretation of literature, it isn't useful on its own for close reading in classrooms.

In the end, multiple valid readings of any written piece are the result. This fact challenges every teacher to present a reasonable approach for arriving at a valid reading of the text. Formalist literary devices provide the foundation for any critical reading of a text and will provide the evidence for students to assemble meaning. Students might then apply one of the critical lenses to establish a valid reading, grounded in solid textual evidence. As teachers work with beginning critical readers, the focus must be solidly on formalist ideas, since this will provide emerging literary critics with the necessary tools to be accurate in their analysis, both in class and on standardized tests.

Having reviewed the historical background of literary criticism and its instructional technique, close reading, let us consider two important factors in bringing this technique to the classroom, its research background and important instructional shifts that close reading helps us meet.

Research Background

In examining the research background on close reading as an instructional strategy, it is useful to define a turning point in interest in the strategy. Prior to the implementation of the CCSS and the subsequent revisions of state standards in non–Common Core states, close reading was not a widely practiced instructional strategy in U.S. secondary schools, and thus "it has not been studied directly through rigorous academic research" (Student Achievement Partners, 2016, p. 10). Since 2005, with changes wrought by the aforementioned revisions of state standards, there has been increased interest in the use of close reading. Luckily, there are encouraging research studies of aspects of close reading that suggest the strategy is highly effective.

Close reading accesses several important aspects of the teaching of reading, most importantly vocabulary and syntax instruction. Further, close reading encourages the development of fluency through its repeated readings of texts, made more broadly effective with its focus on deliberately practicing with complex texts. Researchers K. Anders Ericsson, Ralf T. Krampe, and Clemens Tesch-Römer (1993) have shown that working repeatedly with complex texts, where students have feedback on their progress over extended periods, results in highly developed interpretation skills. An additional area that close reading accesses is the standard of coherence, where closely reading complex texts develops students' appreciation for what texts have to offer. Students who develop a high standard of coherence expect to understand a text deeply and will work to achieve that understanding (Pearson & Liben, 2013).

Researchers have shown the importance of vocabulary development for decades. Betty Hart and Todd R. Risley (1995) studied the effects of poor vocabulary development on students at risk in a study of conversations in the home as the children developed. The study showed that low-socioeconomic families provide fewer exposures to conversation than high-socioeconomic families. In 2003, Hart and Risley published a study including the 1995 information with additional data that demonstrated students from low-socioeconomic families can arrive at age three having been exposed to thirty million fewer words than their high-socioeconomic counterparts. Vocabulary level is directly related to a student's ability to read, as most reading instruction begins by teaching students to decode words on a page (Kamil & Hiebert, 2005). Thus, the vocabulary gap becomes a reading gap. Keith E. Stanovich's (1986) study described the prolonged effects of reading gaps. Poor readers do not make the same progress as strong readers across reading instruction in school, so the reading gap expands. By having them practice close reading as one aspect of a robust reading instruction program, teachers give students the tools to help close these gaps.

In the practice of close reading, students must interact with textual structures at the sentence and paragraph levels. This action develops an understanding of and the ability to analyze syntax, which has been shown to be one of the most challenging analytical elements for students (Nelson, Perfetti, Liben, & Liben, 2012). A strong understanding of syntax has been shown to promote student reading comprehension (Goff, Pratt, & Ong, 2005).

Close reading also requires students to return often to the same text with increasingly closer looks at the elements of the passage. These repeated readings improve fluency, which has been shown to have a direct connection to student reading comprehension (Paige, 2011). Further, the National Reading Panel's (2000) meta-analysis demonstrated the direct connection between repeated readings of the same text and increases in both reading fluency and comprehension.

Instructional Shifts

Instructional shifts in English language arts and mathematics have been identified as implementation of Common Core State Standards and the associated revisions of non-CCSS state standards proceed. In English language arts, these key instructional shifts include (Common Core State Standards Initiative, n.d.):

1. Regular practice with <u>complex texts</u> and their academic language

2. Reading, writing, and speaking <u>grounded in evidence from texts</u>, both literary and informational

3. <u>Building knowledge</u> through content-rich nonfiction

The instructional strategy of close reading is one very powerful method of achieving all these instructional shifts. It provides the additional benefits of increasing vocabulary acquisition, reading fluency, and reading comprehension (Student Achievement Partners, 2016). A 2006 study of the ACT test indicated that students' abilities to work with, comprehend, and analyze complex texts is a strong indicator of college readiness. Useful in most situations, the close reading process has the advantage of being a strong method for practicing analysis, whether by a single student (such as in a testing situation) or, more ideally, in a group situation (such as a class discussion; ACT, 2006). Given that information, close reading is a strategy every teacher should consider using on a regular basis, since the ACT study indicated that only 51 percent of all students who took the ACT in 2005 (and significantly lower proportions of disadvantaged socioeconomic and ethnic groups) demonstrated college readiness in reading (ACT, 2006).

Following is an effective process for teaching close reading, recommended as a way to support these instructional shifts. The following chapters provide more detail on the process.

A Process for Close Reading

Teachers who have used close reading in their classrooms likely will have tried many different methods. The *Introduction to Great Books* (Great Books Foundation, 1990) program informs the process of close reading this book describes. The Great Books Foundation designed, developed, and published this program to provide a framework for students to encounter and enter challenging texts. The following recommended process bears resemblance to their approach, though the discussion process looks considerably different. It is effective for close reading for most students in most classrooms, and students can adapt it for testing situations. The process is effective regardless of the kind of close reading text or content area. As a reminder, the steps in their basic form are as follows.

1. **Prereading:** Answering a question and accessing background knowledge on the close reading passage

2. **Reading twice and annotating:** Reading through the selection twice while annotating potential evidence

3. **Generating questions:** Using annotations to generate questions about the text that are useful in a general discussion or as prompts for the next reading

4. **Reading analytically:** Reading the text analytically a third time, focusing on the questions identified in step 3

5. **Discussing as a class or analyzing individually:** Finalizing the class discussion or individual analysis of the information gathered from step 4

6. **Processing:** Drawing conclusions

Each of the following chapters presents suggestions and teaching strategies for sharing the steps in the process with students and encouraging them to develop and deepen their abilities.

Summary

Close reading is a process of deep investigation into a text and the authorial choices therein. Although formalist ideas provide the method of analysis this book describes, the process is compatible with any number of critical lenses. This allows students to support their responses to a text with the solid evidence of literary devices. In subsequent chapters, we explore a six-step close reading process useful in all content areas. Students who master this process will not only find success in classwork and standardized tests but also develop the critical-thinking abilities essential for the rest of their lives.

Chapter 2

PREREADING

Close reading has the potential of guiding students through analytical thinking, but the very nature of the strategy requires substantial teacher preparation. As a first step in the close reading process, students must answer a question and access background knowledge as preparation for a more in-depth reading. If a teacher asks her students to read deeply, she must have done it herself first. This is not to suggest that a teacher should read the text to establish one correct meaning, but it does mean instructors must be deeply familiar with the text to adequately guide students in close reading, including in the initial step of answering questions and accessing background knowledge. Teachers should carefully select the right text (and the right portion of that text) to meet students' needs and abilities. Once the teacher is prepared for close reading, the students must be as well. They must be familiar with the close reading process before they begin it. The teacher must also design a prereading activity that aligns with the merits of the selected text. Then, the class can begin an effective close reading session. In the sections that follow, we consider the details of text selection, teacher preparation, student introduction to close reading, and prereading activities.

Text Selection

Choosing the correct text is an important consideration before bringing one into the classroom for close reading. This selection is more complex than it may appear at first because, while curricula are well-stocked with potential texts, not all of them are candidates for close reading. Indeed, some texts may not reveal much in close reading, while the complexity of others may frustrate beginning close readers.

There are a few technical factors that are important to consider when choosing a text.

- Student and teacher interest
- Level of complexity
- Type of text
- Passage length and purpose

Student and Teacher Interest

It is not always possible to choose a text that connects with student interests, but it does help to do so when possible, especially in the early stages of developing strong close readers. If students like the style and content of a text, they are likely to engage more as they discover the authorial moves, those choices an author intentionally makes in a text and on which we want our students to focus. If students can learn to closely read texts they enjoy, they can apply the skill to other texts and expand their ideas of what makes a text important and worthy of reading. There are many methods for discovering the interests of students and applying them to the text selection. Early in the school year, a student-background survey might provide a teacher with insights about the activities and interests of his students, and this can be invaluable information as he chooses the texts he will teach.

There are many types of background surveys. See figure 2.1, which exemplifies the types of questions that might be on a survey. Such surveys will reveal much more than the specific interests of students, and teachers can use them in many ways. However, in selecting texts that meet with student interests, the survey information can be invaluable.

- Where were you born?
- How many brothers and sisters do you have?
- What are some things about your family that make you proud?
- What kinds of things did you do over the summer or on vacation that you enjoyed?
- What would you do if you knew you couldn't fail?
- Do you have any hobbies (collecting things, artistic endeavors, building things)? If so, what are they?
- Do you participate in sports? If so, which sports? What do you like best about playing that sport?
- Do you take lessons of any kind (music, art, singing, dance, speech)? If so, what kind?
- What is your favorite book, game, movie, video or computer game, or television show?
- If you had to describe yourself in a sentence or two, what might you say that would help others learn something about your personal interests?
- During my free time I like to _____.
- One thing I really like to do with my friends is _____.
- I really enjoy _____.
- My family enjoys _____.
- If I had a month of Saturdays, I'd spend most of my time _____.
- Someday I'd like to be _____.

Source: Marzano Research, 2016c.

Figure 2.1: Sample survey questions.

Visit **marzanoresearch.com/classroomstrategies** for a free reproducible version of this figure.

In addition to student interest, teacher interest is important when selecting a text. Like any person, teachers love certain texts, those filled with words that jump off the page because of their own close reading and deep engagement. Teachers who bring that enthusiasm to students' interaction with a text are likely to engender some similar level of appreciation in their students. On the other hand, any teacher will have to use texts they find uninspiring, and some of those texts may be ones they are supposed to like. When possible (and it isn't always possible), teachers should avoid selecting these texts for close reading because prejudices are likely to show through as they share the texts with students. As a personal example, I have a lifelong relationship with William Shakespeare, not only as a teacher but also as an actor and a director. When I teach using *Hamlet, Othello, King Lear, Twelfth Night,* and *A Midsummer Night's Dream,* I know my enthusiasm for these master works as a whole and for the numerous short passages I have students close read helps them appreciate the superb level of writing. Yet I avoid teaching *Julius Caesar*, not because I think it is a flawed play, but because I know I would lack the enthusiasm to do it justice. Being careful about one's own feelings in the text selection is important to providing students with the best close reading experience possible.

At the same time, all teachers will encounter situations where required texts fail to inspire them. There are reasons some texts are in the curriculum; at some point, someone saw the value of that text. Teachers might revisit a text with an eye toward finding ways to be enthusiastic about it (or at least appreciate it). Literature teachers might read some literary criticism of the text to help discover its value and support their own growing appreciation of it. Social studies teachers could review the historical moment of a text or read an expert analysis of its impact to perhaps change their opinions. Teachers of any subject area can converse with colleagues about ways to connect with a text. When dealing with an uninspiring text, teachers should do their best to prevent their biases from impacting students' experiences with that work.

Level of Complexity

Although student interest is an important factor, so is the level of complexity. The text must appropriately challenge students to increase their reading and analytical abilities (McKeown, Beck, & Blake, 2009). Obviously, students just starting to learn the close reading process need to practice it with less challenging texts. As students improve in their abilities to read closely, as measured by a proficiency scale, teachers will want to present them with ever more challenging texts. (See chapter 6, page 87, for more about proficiency scales.)

An important consideration is the reading level of the text. Tradition sometimes dictates that certain texts are taught at a certain grade level, perhaps without due consideration of the text's reading level. Here is an example of a challenging text traditionally taught in either seventh or eighth grade:

> It's a wonder I haven't abandoned all my ideals, they seem so absurd and impractical. Yet I cling to them because I still believe, in spite of everything, that people are truly good at heart. It's utterly impossible for me to build my life on a foundation of chaos, suffering and death. I see the world being slowly transformed into a wilderness, I hear the approaching thunder that, one day, will destroy us too, I feel the suffering of millions. And yet, when I look up at the sky, I somehow feel that everything will change for the better, that this cruelty will end, that peace and tranquility will return once more. —July 15, 1944 (Frank, 1947/1997, pp. 12–13)

This excerpt from Anne Frank's *The Diary of a Young Girl* will be familiar to many. Though a traditional middle school text, its reading level is tenth grade (Flesch-Kincaid 10.2). Flesch-Kincaid reports readability at typical grade levels for U.S. public schools. This is not to say teachers shouldn't teach the book in middle school, but it does demonstrate why many middle school students struggle to understand the text. When choosing texts, teachers should start with a clear understanding of students' abilities and decide whether to connect with their current reading level or challenge them a bit to go beyond it. Further, it is important to examine texts traditionally taught at each grade level and understand the challenge each work represents to readers in each grade. It's possible some texts should be taught at higher grade levels than they are, while others, though above the grade level, stay there for other important pedagogical reasons (such as preparing students for the next level of instruction). A good example is Shakespeare's (1595/1997b) *Romeo and Juliet*. This text, traditionally taught to ninth graders, represents a reading level far beyond ninth grade. For example, the opening prologue speech, a Shakespearean sonnet, has a Flesch-Kincaid reading level of 14.2, which suggests its reading level is second-year college. Yet it is an important text to teach in the first year of high school to introduce students to the complexities of Shakespearean writing as preparation for other forms of that writing in the years ahead. Recognizing that the text is very challenging to ninth-grade readers would suggest to teachers that asking students to independently read and understand the entire play is probably beyond their abilities. Thus, we approach a complex text such as *Romeo and Juliet* in a different manner, often reading portions of it rather than the entire text.

At the same time, teachers should not be afraid of presenting students with complicated passages that challenge their understanding and appreciation of a writer's craft. In close reading, the focus is on an author's style and craft in addition to content. In a high-quality text, the author's craft will support and inform the content. One may read a classical author for many reasons, and often those reasons are related to content—though style should not be ignored. Virginia Woolf, the amazing early–20th century British writer, is often seen as an important feminist movement writer, and rightly so, but one should not ignore the stylistic power of an author who can craft writing like this:

> Strife, divisions, difference of opinion, prejudices twisted into the very fibre of being, oh, that they should begin so early, Mrs. Ramsay deplored. They were so critical, her children. They talked such nonsense. She went from the dining-room, holding James by the hand, since he would not go with the others. It seemed to her such nonsense—inventing differences, when people, heaven knows, were different enough without that. The real differences, she thought, standing by the drawing-room window, are enough, quite enough. She had in mind at the moment, rich and poor, high and low; the great in birth receiving from her, half grudgingly, some respect, for had she not in her veins the blood of that very noble, if slightly mythical, Italian house, whose daughters, scattered about English drawing-rooms in the nineteenth century, had lisped so charmingly, had stormed so wildly, and all her wit and her bearing and her temper came from them, and not from the sluggish English, or the cold Scotch; but more profoundly, she ruminated the other problem, of rich and poor, and the things she saw with her own eyes, weekly, daily, here or in London, when she visited this widow, or that struggling wife in person with a bag on her arm, and a note-book and pencil with which she wrote down in columns carefully ruled for the purpose wages and spendings, employment and unemployment, in the hope that thus she would cease to be a private woman whose charity was half a sop to her own indignation, half a relief to her own curiosity, and become what with her untrained mind she greatly admired, an investigator, elucidating the social problem. (Woolf, 1927/1989, pp. 8–9)

The complexities of this passage are enormous. On first reading, one notices rather readily the content, which describes the main character and her internal thoughts—first about her children, then the issue of her own social acceptance, and finally the larger social issues of the time. But that is not what is vital in this passage. Woolf's ability to present layer upon layer of ideas folded one within another, represented through complex sentences that enfold clauses within clauses, challenges the reader and thus represents the complexity of the main character. One cannot ignore the quality of this writing; few writers can emulate it. While such a passage would be a challenge to even the most diligent high school seniors, it is something teachers should occasionally expose their students to so they can appreciate what good writing is. Such writing does not primarily entertain; it is artistically exquisite.

There are several methods for teachers to assess a text's reading level and complexity level to match the needs of students. Reading level is a good starting point, and many textbook publishers provide this information in their catalogs and on their websites. Teachers can also establish the reading level of a text by typing (or copying and pasting) a segment of text into Microsoft Word. Microsoft Word, with its Spelling and Grammar tool, can help teachers assess many readability factors and help teachers judge whether a text is appropriate for their students. The following applies to Word 2016, but similar settings are available in most previous versions of the program. In Windows, start by accessing your File menu and then clicking Options. Under the section When Correcting for Spelling and Grammar, be sure to select Show Readability Statistics. Once in the document, click on the Review menu and click Spelling and Grammar. On a Mac, start by accessing Preferences. In the Spelling and Grammar section, select Show Readability Statistics. Then, in the Tools menu, click Spelling and Grammar. At the end of the spelling and grammar check, Word will display the Flesch-Kincaid level of the highlighted text. Another easy way to check a text's reading level is with the website Readable.io (https://readable.io). Here you can type or copy and paste a section of text into the website and receive information about its reading level through several methods, including Flesch-Kincaid.

Text complexity is much more challenging to determine. Lexile or ATOS measurements can provide good estimates of text complexity, though they may not address all possible interpretations of a text. Thus, the best advice for teachers is to use their best judgment given the goals of the close reading session and their own experience with the text. If the text is at an appropriate reading level, teachers should determine whether the text provides students a rich experience in using authorial devices (we will discuss this more later) and presenting ideas. Making this determination is not an exact science, but a teacher's experience of teaching a text is the best determinant of whether the text is at the correct level of complexity. If you are new to the content you're teaching, seek out the advice of teachers who have taught the same texts for years.

Type of Text

Most academic standards (including the CCSS) look at texts in two categories: (1) literary and (2) informational. This distinction in the standards suggests a fundamental difference between these two kinds of texts. The reason for this distinction is to promote the teaching of informational texts in public school classrooms (Common Core State Standards Initiative, n.d.). This is a vitally important effort because standards-defined informational text is the most common form of text students encounter throughout their lives. That being said, the dichotomy between literary and informational texts is a false one.

Many people typically think of literature as works of creative writing, often fiction or poetry that evoke an emotional response from the reader. Literary texts use characterization, plot, and figurative language to great effect. Rhetoric, the art of persuasion, is the basis for informational text. That statement may be surprising, but any text presents a rhetorical stance, an inherent argument for the reader. For example, a text may appear to do nothing but inform, stating a series of facts. However, selecting those facts, choosing their presentation in a particular sequence, and selecting any textual structures presents an argument in favor of the information, and a careful reader can see them in that manner. When students analytically read an informational text, this can reveal authorial choices related to the author's purpose and occasion, each of which are related to the creation of an argument and a reaction in the mind of the reader. *Rhetoric* is essentially the skill of argumentation, or the ability to use an appeal to build a strong and convincing argument. Already one can see the separate concepts and terminology typically associated with each category of texts. However, if one backs away from the dichotomy of informational and literary and sees a text as a text only, then one can perceive more commonality between these two categories. For example, what literary critics call *figurative language* (simply put, the ability to say one thing and mean at least two things) is really a *rhetorical figure*, a method used both in literary and informational texts. To illustrate, Robert Burns (1794) begins his famous poem with, "My love is like a red, red rose." This is figurative language, specifically a simile, in which two dissimilar things—(1) his love and (2) a rose—are compared using the word *like*. Although literary critics call such devices figurative language, the larger category to which figurative language belongs is the category of rhetorical figures, and writers of argument make effective use of such structures. Many aspects of literary texts have their counterparts in informational texts. For example, there is much commonality, if not a one-to-one correspondence, between the basic elements of *setting* in a literary text and *occasion* in an informational one. For this reason, consider simplifying instruction in these areas, and when possible, approach teaching both the literary and informational elements together. That way, students can see these connections and apply similar techniques to both literary and informational texts immediately.

This may oppose the traditional approach of *genre-based units* (a unit on the short story and then a later unit on informational text in an English language arts classroom, or a narrative story in one unit and an essay in another unit in a physical education classroom). However, teaching the application of rhetorical elements to both kinds of texts reveals a new form of intertextual instruction, where students might read a short story on a topic and then an essay on the same general topic within a few days.

The advantage is that teachers can focus less on genre and more on text complexity as students develop close reading skills. Thus, a class can start with approachable, grade-level short stories, poems, and essays and then proceed to much more challenging texts without getting caught up in the type (genre) of text. This is more efficient in developing student skills and is wholly appropriate when the focus is on developing students' close reading and interpretive skills.

This same approach can apply in content areas other than English language arts. For example, a social studies teacher examining the historical period in 18th century England might have students examine a satirical work of prose, such as Jonathan Swift's (1729/1996) *A Modest Proposal*, as a text supporting the Irish rebellion against English landlords, as well as some of the satirical poetry on the same subject. In the same way, a science teacher might have students read an essay on environmental issues, and then turn to the more elegant prose of, for example, conservationist Rachel Carson, understanding that her work is still an informational text but filled with effective literary devices.

To be clear, we cannot teach the skill of close reading of informational text solely by providing students with literary texts, or the reverse. The skills of close reading are the same, regardless of which type of text a student reads. We must teach students *all* types of texts, and we must do a thorough job of preparing them to handle complex and challenging informational texts, because these are the primary texts they will encounter in postsecondary education and in life.

Passage Length and Purpose

Ideally, the passage should be rich and short. A close reading passage should offer a great deal from a small amount of text. For this reason, teachers must be aware that not everything is a candidate for close reading. Reading through an entire scene of a Shakespearean tragedy or even half a chapter of a grade-level novel is simply too much text for close reading, especially for students in lower secondary grades. It should be possible to provide the entire text for a close reading passage on a single side of an 8.5 × 11 sheet of paper. If the text requires multiple pages, consider shortening it; there is probably too much there to deal with effectively. The aim is for students to delve deeply into the text; the more text, the shallower the dig.

While it is true that different students will notice different things, the shorter the selection (within reason), the more likely there will be commonality among the students' annotations. So, it is in the teacher's hands to find that one passage, perhaps just a few sentences or a couple of paragraphs at most, that yields the most in terms of meaning, literary devices, argument development, or the focus of the lesson.

At the same time, it is occasionally necessary to use a passage that is much longer due to the nature of the study in a unit. It may be, for example, an important historical document that demands longer sections for analysis. An example of this appears in appendix B (page 107), which examines an excerpt from Thucydides's (431–404 BCE/1972) *History of the Peloponnesian War*, specifically, Pericles's Funeral Oration. This superb speech does not lend itself to short passages; it is so finely crafted that students must look at a longer-than-usual excerpt to see the way the author linked many elements of argument together. There are times when students should work with longer passages, but teachers must limit those occasions and be sure to provide adequate class time for them to go deeply into the longer passages.

As we attempt to determine a short, specific passage from a larger text as the subject of close reading, there are four general guidelines to follow.

1. Be sure the text is appropriate to the class level. Obviously, we want the reading level and complexity to be appropriate for the current overall abilities of the class.

2. The text should be relevant to the content of the lesson or unit. The lesson or unit may have a focus on a particular theme or literary device. The passage should be rich in this element.

3. Be sure that the length of the text fits its purpose. The purpose of the lesson may dictate how long the passage can be. If we're looking for only an example or two of a particular device, then the passage can be substantially shorter than if we're looking to determine the effect of multiple uses of a device.

4. Ensure that the style of the text fits its purpose. Different writing styles present different challenges to students. If the purpose of the lesson or unit is to focus on a specific, challenging style for analysis, then the style should match that purpose. If the purpose of the lesson or unit is to focus on a specific rhetorical device and its use, then the style should support (not challenge) the development of analysis of that skill.

The following is an example of how a teacher might select a short passage. Shakespeare's (1595/1997b) *Romeo and Juliet* is standard fare in a ninth-grade English language arts classroom. As stated previously, it is impossible for students to close read an entire play, or even full scenes from a Shakespearean play, at this grade level. Assume a teacher has planned a three-week unit on *Romeo and Juliet* and will not be asking students to read every word of the play. Some of the less important scenes can be viewed on video in between readings of important scenes. In a three-week unit, the class might close read three or four passages. Which scenes the teacher chooses depends largely on the focus and purpose of the study of the play. First, the teacher identifies a list of potential scenes from which she will choose close reading passages. The four guidelines provided in the preceding list make it easier to identify potential passages. Some vital scenes that might contain close reading passages include the following.

- Act 1, scene 1 (the opening scene with the brawl in the street)

- Act 1, scene 4 (Mercutio's Queen Mab speech)

- Act 2, scene 2 (the first long exchange between Romeo and Juliet)

- Act 3, scene 1 (the fight that causes Romeo to intervene)

- Act 3, scene 2 (Juliet's "Gallop apace" speech)

- Act 5, scene 3 (the final scene, which includes the deaths of Romeo and Juliet)

Of course, there are many more scenes that might be added to this list. All or any of these would offer good selections for close reading. However, the teacher decides to look closer at act 1, scene 4, and particularly at Mercutio's famous Queen Mab speech. In *The Riverside Shakespeare* (Evans & Tobin, 1997), the Queen Mab speech in act 1, scene 4 is forty-one lines long. Though it is possible to close read the entire speech, it is lengthy, so the teacher decides to select a shorter passage to ask students to analyze deeply. Each reader will bring a different perspective to the table that will color the interpretation of the elements (see the section Teacher Preparation). Considering the subject matter of the passage, the teacher identifies two reasons why the passage appears in the play as justification for having students consider the passage. One reason is that Shakespeare uses this passage to develop the character of Mercutio, a friend of Romeo's who is easily drawn into excess, spirit, and anger, thus aligning with the meaning of his name as one who is changeable. Another reason for the speech is to comment on the nature of dreams, which both Romeo and Mercutio claim they have experienced recently in the scene. In the speech, Mercutio supports his earlier claim, "Dreamers often lie." He initially wishes to make fun of Romeo's intense sadness over the loss of his first love in the play, Rosaline. Over the course of the speech, Mercutio becomes quickly agitated, starting by kidding Romeo about the influence of the fairies in his dream and ending by being filled with anger at the power of dreams to unmask hidden emotions in many people.

To choose one piece of this speech, the teacher starts by considering the academic purpose of asking students to close read the speech. If the purpose is to focus on Shakespeare's ability to quickly and effectively develop imagery in his poetry, the first section describing how Queen Mab arrives would be a good candidate. If the focus is on the *mercurial* nature of Mercutio and tracking the changes in his emotions across the speech, the second half (when he begins to work himself into agitation) would be a good candidate. The teacher could also use the checklists later in the chapter (pages 26–27) to help determine the right focus.

Assume the teacher wants to focus on Shakespeare's abilities to use imagery. She first narrows the long speech into the section that deals specifically with that developing imagery, lines 1–17:

MERCUTIO
O, then, I see Queen Mab hath been with you.
She is the fairies' midwife, and she comes
In shape no bigger than an agate-stone
On the forefinger of an alderman,
Drawn with a team of little atomi
Over men's noses as they lie asleep.
Her chariot is an empty hazel-nut,
Made by the joiner squirrel or old grub,
Time out a' mind the fairies' coachmakers.
Her waggon-spokes made of long spinners' legs,
The cover of the wings of grasshoppers,
Her traces of the smallest spider web,
Her collars of the moonshine's wat'ry beams,
Her whip of cricket's bone, the lash of film,
Her waggoner a small grey-coated gnat,
Not half so big as a round little worm
Prick'd from the lazy finger of a maid.
(Shakespeare, 1595/1997b, p. 1111)

This would make a fine text for close reading. However, a teacher might decide to focus students' attention on an even narrower section. This would require and enable them to look very closely at a short piece of text. The following is an example of an imagery-filled segment of the previous selection:

Her traces of the smallest spider web,
Her collars of the moonshine's wat'ry beams,

Her whip of cricket's bone, the lash of film,
Her waggoner a small grey-coated gnat,
Not half so big as a round little worm
Prick'd from the lazy finger of a maid.

These six lines will serve the same academic purpose as the seventeen-line segment but will focus the students' reading much more narrowly on a small amount of text rich in imagery—the very device the teacher wishes students to examine. In this way, teachers can make informed decisions about the correct length of text given the academic purpose of the close reading activity.

What happens once a teacher chooses a close reading passage? Of course, she must prepare to share it with students.

Teacher Preparation

As mentioned previously, close reading a passage in preparation for teaching it to students does not consist of finding the *right answer* (although students, if they correctly implement the close reading process, may arrive at the same conclusions as their teacher). Close reading exposes the basic authorial moves and textual elements at work in a text. You can assess the accuracy of that information. But from that foundation, each reader will bring to the analysis a different perspective that will color the interpretation of those elements. The section on the history of literary criticism (see chapter 1, page 7) describes examples of ideological lenses that may find their way into student interpretations, and there are many more as well. Teachers should be open to those interpretations, provided the interpretations are grounded in a solid close reading of the text. Judging interpretation is an important part of teaching close reading. The teacher must be open-minded and, at the same time, analytical. This stance is vital in the classroom; students need to see that their teacher is open to their ideas, but they should not assume that anything goes.

Next, we examine some other potential issues in preparing a close reading lesson. Every teacher comes to the profession on a different road. Some may have solid backgrounds in close reading, others will be learning with their students, and many will be in between. Teachers who do not have much experience with close reading can still teach close reading to their students. As adults, their judgment will be better than their students', and careful preparation will allow teachers to lead the process well. At the same time, teachers who are experienced close readers can still learn from their students. Many minds deeply reading a text will discover new things, even when the teacher has years of experience with the text, and he or she must be open to those discoveries.

The remainder of this section describes textual elements teachers can look for as they close read a passage in preparation for teaching it. As such, if you are an experienced close reader and confident in your own abilities, you may wish to skip this material. If you are new to close reading or are looking for a structured approach to your own close reading of a text, you may find the following suggestions helpful.

During their own close reading as part of the preparation stage, teachers will primarily be concerned with the reading, annotating, and analyzing steps. As they carry out these steps, teachers can use the checklists in figures 2.2 (page 26) and 2.3 (page 27) as guides. Figure 2.2 contains a checklist of things to look for when analyzing a passage of literary text (broken down for prose and drama versus poetry), and figure 2.3 contains a checklist for informational text. However, teachers should consider each item, even if it appears in the list for another type of writing. Many prose writers use poetic devices; dramatists will venture into poetry, and informational texts use these devices as well. So, although the checklist is divided into sections, never feel bound by those divisions. The section on literary and rhetorical devices in chapter 3 (page 50) provides details on some of these devices.

Prose and Drama	Poetry
☐ Setting	☐ Setting
☐ Point of view	☐ Point of view
☐ Grammar	☐ Title
☐ Diction	☐ Diction
☐ Sound devices	☐ Imagery
☐ Syntax	☐ Symbolism
☐ Figurative language	☐ Irony
☐ Irony	☐ Allusion
☐ Tone	☐ Sound devices
☐ Theme	☐ Figurative language
	☐ Tone
	☐ Tonal shifts
	☐ Shifts in time and place
	☐ Changes in line or stanza length
	☐ Ironic shifts
	☐ Poetic structure

Figure 2.2: Checklist for literary texts.

Visit **marzanoresearch.com/classroomstrategies** for a free reproducible version of this figure.

Few passages will use every device listed in a category, but a careful reader should consider whether each device is at work in the text. As a close reader, one must look for two things: (1) where an author obviously and directly uses a device for effect, and (2) where an author uses a pattern of these devices. Teachers, like their students, need to train themselves to look not only for *what* an author is doing but also for *how* and *why* the author is doing it. It is insufficient to simply note that an author uses a specific literary device; what is essential is the effect the device produces. How does an author achieve an effect, and why would he or she do it? Teachers need to push themselves as they prepare for close reading, and they certainly need to push their students to answer these important and deep questions.

Informational Texts		
☐ Occasion	☐ Time ☐ Place ☐ Context	
☐ Purpose	☐ What does the author want from the reader?	
☐ Point of view	☐ First person ☐ Third person	
☐ Style	☐ Grammar	
	☐ Diction	
	☐ Sound devices	
	☐ Syntax	
	☐ Figurative language	
☐ The three appeals	☐ Logos	
	☐ Ethos	
	☐ Pathos	
☐ Argument	☐ Claim	
	☐ Grounds	
	☐ Backing	
	☐ Qualifiers	
☐ Tone and tonal shifts	☐ Diction ☐ Syntax ☐ Imagery ☐ Figurative language	
☐ Theme	☐ Subject matter ☐ Author's attitude	

Figure 2.3: Checklist for informational texts.

Visit **marzanoresearch.com/classroomstrategies** for a free reproducible version of this figure.

As an example, consider the following short passage from the opening of Charles Dickens's (1853/1977) novel *Bleak House*. Keep in mind these are the opening words of a novel that, in the

Norton Critical Edition, goes on for 765 pages. As practice, you can close read this passage using the prose and drama checklist (figure 2.2, page 26):

> London. Michaelmas Term lately over, and the Lord Chancellor sitting in Lincoln's Inn Hall. Implacable November weather. As much mud in the streets, as if the waters had but newly retired from the face of the earth, and it would not be wonderful to meet a Megalosaurus, forty feet long or so, waddling like an elephantine lizard up Holborn Hill. Smoke lowering down from chimney-pots, making a soft black drizzle, with flakes of soot in it as big as full-grown snowflakes—gone into mourning, one might imagine, for the death of the sun. Dogs, undistinguishable in mire. Horses, scarcely better; splashed to their very blinkers. Foot passengers jostling one another's umbrellas, in a general infection of ill-temper, and losing their foot-hold at street-corners, where tens of thousands of other foot passengers have been slipping and sliding since the day broke (if the day ever broke), adding new deposits to the crust upon crust of mud, sticking at those points tenaciously to the pavement, and accumulating at compound interest.
>
> Fog everywhere. Fog up the river, where it flows among green aits and meadows; fog down the river, where it rolls defiled among the tiers of shipping and the waterside pollutions of a great (and dirty) city. Fog on the Essex marshes, fog on the Kentish heights. Fog creeping into the cabooses of collier-brigs, fog lying out on the yards, and hovering in the rigging of great ships; fog drooping on the gunwales of barges and small boats. Fog in the eyes and throats of ancient Greenwich pensioners, wheezing by the firesides of their wards; fog in the stem and bowl of the afternoon pipe of the wrathful skipper, down in his close cabin; fog cruelly pinching the toes and fingers of his shivering little 'prentice boy on deck. Chance people on the bridges peeping over the parapets into a nether sky of fog, with fog all round them, as if they were up in a balloon, and hanging in the misty clouds. (Dickens, 1853/1977, p. 5)

These are only the first two paragraphs, and establishing a foggy setting continues in the novel for some time. Eventually the text evolves into connecting the fog-laden streets with the fog-laden courtroom of Temple Bar, the highest court in Britain, which will be the foggy setting of much of the novel. Focusing just on this short passage, however, the close reader must ask, "What is Dickens doing, and why?"

Some early observations might be that Dickens uses lots of sentence fragments in the opening paragraph of this passage, accompanied by some very long, very cumbersome sentences, especially in paragraph two. The imagery is around dullness, muddiness, and, above all, fog. These are strong initial observations, but close readers must take them to the next level. In other words, ask, "Why would Dickens do that?" or a more detailed phrasing of that question, "What effect does his use of varied syntax and specific imagery have in this passage, and why might he want to create that effect?"

Consider the varied syntax. *Syntax*, among other things, refers to the pattern of sentence types and lengths an author uses in the passage. One type of syntax Dickens uses is a sentence fragment, as in the following examples (Dickens, 1853/1977, p. 5).

- "London."

- "Implacable November weather."

- "Dogs, undistinguishable in mire."

The effect of these fragments is to inform the reader of some images present in the setting at the start of the novel. Opening with the single word *London* suggests a series of well-known images in the reader's imagination. This first statement needs no further information—the single word suffices. Dickens goes on to refine the imagery with more information, spottily, slowly, and then he forces the reader into gradually defining *where* and *when* as the novel begins; it is rather difficult work in the first few sentences. Things gradually appear—as if out of a fog. So, the syntax here (with help from the imagery of mud, dullness, and fog) is serving to establish the setting.

To understand Dickens's deeper purpose as he opens this novel, it is useful to know that the novel will (at least on one level of the story) center on the main adjudicates in the decades-long suit known as *Jarndyce and Jarndyce*. Little happens in the legal proceedings through much of the novel, and it is as difficult to understand the issues in the suit as it is to define the setting through the fog in the streets of London. So, the repetition of *fog* in numerous places in the second paragraph establishes not only setting but also tone for the novel.

It is important to note that the teacher does not necessarily need to identify and analyze everything happening in a close reading passage. It is certainly important, however, that the teacher become responsible for the basics of the text. Students will have questions, and the teacher needs to be familiar enough with the text to answer them. At the same time, the teacher won't (and doesn't need to) catch everything. Students will sometimes notice devices or effects the teacher has not, and this is not a bad thing.

Teachers must directly introduce the close reading process to students, just like any skill.

Student Introduction to Close Reading

Before we can ask students to apply the process effectively with any text, students must understand the need for it and how to effectively use it.

Why Should We Close Read?

Adolescents often fail to grasp the need for a complex process in any undertaking, particularly in activities they perceive as intuitive, such as writing and reading. Students are often amazed to discover that authors spend weeks, even months, perfecting their work through drafting, editing, and rewriting nearly every word. Students often believe writing is either something you can or can't do, and those who can do it often just sit and write, producing eloquent and carefully crafted writing in the first draft. Nothing could be further from reality, but students often don't see this.

The same issue is often true of reading. Students often believe reading is just working through the words and developing an understanding of what is happening. That might be true for beginning reading, but it doesn't constitute deep reading. Of course, students may not appreciate this, and that is where teachers must start in introducing the close reading process.

In developing students' appreciation for why they should close read, it is often effective to begin by presenting them with a very short passage. For grade 6 or grade 7 readers, a teacher might use something familiar to them, like the opening of J. R. R. Tolkien's (1974) *The Hobbit*:

> In a hole in the ground there lived a hobbit. Not a nasty, dirty, wet hole, filled with the ends of worms and an oozy smell, nor yet a dry, bare, sandy hole with nothing in it to sit down on or to eat: it was a hobbit-hole, and that means comfort. (p. 15)

If a teacher asks students to simply read these two opening sentences, react to them, and find everything they can about them, students might well produce some of the following observations.

- Is designed to describe a setting

- Has the feeling of strong description

- Introduces a word the reader might not know—*hobbit*

It is likely students will limit their reactions to these kinds of thoughts. There isn't anything wrong with that, but the goal is to show them there is so much more happening in this short passage than they will see with a surface-level reading. The teacher might follow up by asking questions like the following about the passage.

- "Why might the author start this book with such a short paragraph—just two sentences?"

- "Why is the first sentence very short and the second very long? What does that do to the reader's reaction?"

- "What kind of imagery is the author using here, and what effect does it have?"

- "Who is narrating, and what do we know about that narrator? Do we believe what the narrator is saying? Why? Do we like the narrator or not? Why?"

- "What is the effect of the contrast found in the second sentence? Why does the author put that contrast in the second sentence of the novel? What purpose might he have?"

- "What do we know about hobbits from reading the opening paragraph? How do we know?"

The list of questions could continue, but the point is there are lots of additional things going on, if you know the questions to ask. That is vital—one's reading of a text is only as good as the questions one asks and the answers one generates.

A teacher might use a different text for high school students, but they might read quickly and dismiss the text as relatively unimportant. One of the most famous opening sentences in all of English literature is also the first paragraph of the novel:

> It is a truth universally acknowledged, that a single man in possession of a good fortune, must be in want of a wife. (Austen, 1813/1995, p. 1)

Even if students have never heard of Jane Austen or *Pride and Prejudice*, this sentence will nearly always draw some kind of response. Students read and consider the sentence and react. They might respond with the following.

- The writing has an "in-your-face" kind of feeling.

- It is pretty formal writing.

- They don't agree with the statement—it isn't really "universally acknowledged."

Again, by presenting a series of questions like the following, the teacher can show students they can go deeper.

- "Why would this one sentence make up the entire first paragraph of the novel? What is the author achieving by doing that?"

- "Who is the narrator? Is the narrator male or female? How do you know? Does it matter?"

- "Why did the author choose the verb *must*? What is the effect of doing that?"

- "What is the tone of the sentence? Is it meant literally or satirically? How do we know?"

- "What is the effect of starting with the clause 'It is a truth universally acknowledged'? Why would the author do that? What if, like some of you stated, you disagree?"

- "Why choose the word *want*? What effect does that have?"

- "What would you expect the subject of the novel that follows to be? How do you know?"

Of course, there are many more questions to ask, and that is the point students should understand from this introductory exercise.

After being introduced to close reading with an exercise like the preceding examples, students might suggest that this constitutes overreading the text. Almost inevitably, someone will argue that the author couldn't have intended the reader to read that closely. In response, the teacher might suggest the student consider the assumption of his or her claim—that what the author *intends* is the proper reading of the text. Of course, the reader can't ever know what the author intends. If authorial intention is the standard and the standard is unknown, then we can never know when we're reading at the level we should. The teacher might next ask, "If the text begins to reveal something, and we find support with proper analysis of the text, does this create a valid reading?" The answer to this question is *yes*. If there is solid textual evidence to support an interpretation, then the reading is valid. This may prompt a discussion of literary analysis theory, which may be productive if it is relevant to the students and the course material. In general, it is important to dispel the myth of overreading when introducing close reading in order to prevent this argument from becoming an excuse that students use to stay on the surface of a text or avoid risky ideas.

Once students understand that they can and should delve deeper into the text, the discussion can then turn to how exactly close reading is done.

How Do We Close Read?

Teachers should directly teach students the close reading process before they ask students to use it on a passage. This eliminates some confusion and allows students to orient themselves to the steps in the process. The following sections detail each step and how teachers can explain or model it for students.

Step 1: Prereading

The first step in the close reading process is to encounter the text in a basic way before moving to deeper reading. The essence of *prereading* is to make every effort to engage with a first reading of the text by accessing background knowledge.

In a whole-class situation, teachers will provide opportunities for students to think about the subject matter of a passage by asking them to consider their own viewpoints on the topic or what they already know about it. This step can also consist of activities with an obvious or more obscure connection to the text to pique students' interest. Prereading can also involve skimming the text in a series of steps that help students gain a very general understanding of the topic. Organized skimming is perhaps most helpful in preparing students when they do not have the benefit of teacher guidance. When students come to a text completely cold, as in their own personal reading or when encountering a passage on a test, they can use the following guidelines to self-assess their own involvement with the subject.

- Look carefully at the title (if any) and consider your own thoughts about the implied subject.

- Read the introduction (if any—they're often on standardized tests) and think carefully about what you already know about the implied subject.

- Scan through the passage, getting a feeling for the subject in a very general sense. Ask yourself things you already know about the subject.

- Read the first sentence of each paragraph to get a feeling for the development of the passage. Again, assess the indicated subject.

Important questions for students to ask themselves during and after this process include the following.

- "What do I already know about the subject?"

- "What is implied about the subject that I didn't already know?"

- "What feelings do I have about this information I am about to read?"

- "After scanning the passage and thinking about it, what questions do I have?"

These questions are very general, but they will lead students to a quick assessment of their own understanding and interest. As a starting point for encountering a text, it will at least generate some interest, however minimal.

Step 2: Reading Twice and Annotating

We address specific annotation skills in chapter 3 (page 41), but when introducing the process to students, modeling one form of reading twice and annotating will give students an idea of what they will be asked to do later. Consider the passage from *Pride and Prejudice* (Austen, 1813/1995) the teacher used to introduce students to the need for close reading:

> It is a truth universally acknowledged, that a single man in possession of a good fortune, must be in want of a wife. (p. 1)

In modeling the process, the teacher starts with a first reading and demonstrates the reaction of a reader encountering the passage for the first and second times by speaking through the process as described below. He also models annotating the passage.

> *After a quick reading of the sentence, my first reaction is: it is a bold statement that is funny, though I'm not sure I agree with it. So, what makes it funny? One idea might be that there is a tension between the supposedly "universal" nature of the sentence the opening clause creates and my own reaction. As a reader, I'm not sure I am part of that "universal acknowledgment"! So, as I first annotate, I want to mark "universally acknowledged" with the explanation I just said—that I disagree. As I return to read the sentence the second time, I want to focus on what I haven't noticed, particularly the second portion of the sentence.*
>
> *This time, the most important word in the second half of the sentence is the word must. It just sort of stuck out for me. So, I will annotate that, but then I have to know why it stuck out. So, I make a question, Why is the word must important? Well, it implies that something has to happen. But it isn't true that if a single man has a good fortune, he has to be looking for a wife. So, why does the author say that? The effect is that the statement goes against reality, so it is funny, and perhaps it is satirical. Now I have some annotations for the next portion of the process.*

Figure 2.4 depicts the teacher's annotations.

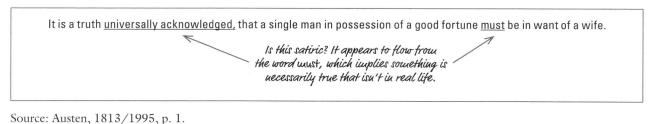

Source: Austen, 1813/1995, p. 1.

Figure 2.4: Sample annotations.

Step 3: Generating Questions

After reading twice and annotating, the next step is to use those annotations to create questions. In the classroom, students can work together to discuss and generate questions; on a standardized test or other situation where no discussion is permitted, students can complete this step individually. *Generating questions* simply means rephrasing annotations into questions that will inform the next reading, or the deeply analytical close reading.

Using the teacher's modeled annotations in figure 2.4, the questions might be as follows.

1. Is the sentence satirical?

2. If it is satirical, why would the author open the book with satire?

3. If it is not satirical, why would the author open the book with a statement that is clearly not true?

With these questions in mind, the class can turn to the next step in the close reading process.

Step 4: Reading Analytically

At this stage, the teacher returns to the opening sentence with the three questions in mind. Analysis is the heart of the close reading process, and the reader examines textual evidence in order to answer questions. In modeling the analytical reading of the text, the teacher might share his thoughts with students as follows.

> In deciding whether the sentence is satirical, we have to keep in mind the purpose of satire—to make fun of something in society that the writer feels might be a problem and needs changing. It is not clear from a single sentence that there is a problem here, but there are hints—this subject matter hints at the problems single men with good fortunes have—lots of single women after them! So, we have to decide whether the passage is satire or not. Probably it is because the author opens the book with it, and it is clearly not literally true. The author wouldn't put that statement first if it was meant to be taken literally. So, assuming that we are working with satire, what else can we note that constitutes evidence of satire at work? Focusing on the words present in the sentence, we've dealt with all of the important ones except want. That word suggests a need—something that a person must have to be OK in the world, to survive, either physically, mentally, or socially. Of course, the idea that people need to get married isn't true either, so this is likely more evidence that the sentence is satirical. Going past the words on the page, the diction, we have no imagery to deal with except perhaps "good fortune," though that seems vague in terms of generating a vision of a good fortune. Turning to the syntax of the passage, we have a single sentence that constitutes the entire first paragraph of the novel. It is a compound-complex sentence, but it does not depict a deeply convoluted idea. In fact, the statement is very easy to understand with just a few moments of thought. So, the effect of that syntactic choice, of a single sentence with a clear idea constituting the opening paragraph, suggests that the author wanted the reader to read that sentence, and then stop and think about it for a moment before going on to the next paragraph, and that fits with the sentence being satirical. A single statement of satire, introducing the subject of fortunes and marriage, not only provides an entrance into the subject matter of the novel but also does so in a way that sets a satirical tone.

Step 5: Discussing as a Class or Analyzing Individually

When the whole class is engaged in a close reading activity, this step allows students to share their discoveries from step 4, challenge each other to present evidence, draw further conclusions, and so on. When students are close reading alone (as on a test), they can use this step to recheck their evidence, integrate multiple ideas, and so on. In modeling the annotation process in step 4, the teacher has also modeled the individual analysis process of step 5. When introducing students to the close reading process, it is up to the teacher whether or not to model the class discussion phase. It may not be necessary, depending on the length of the sample passage and students' familiarity with group discussion.

Step 6: Using Processing Activities

This involves using the conclusions from the analysis steps to answer test questions or complete another activity. To introduce this step, the teacher can return to some of the key reasons for using the close reading process—developing a deep reading of a passage is inherently rewarding, and students will be impressed with what they discover about a single sentence of a novel. Additionally, close reading is a useful skill in many situations in life, such as responding to editorials, reacting to instructions and policy statements of employers, and in responding to political ads. At this point, the teacher might ask students to imagine encountering this sentence as a reading passage on standardized test. He might present them with the sample test questions in figure 2.5. It isn't necessary to have students complete the test, though some certainly might. The key here is to demonstrate to students that after practicing the close reading process on the sentence, they can answer any or all of these questions confidently and effectively.

Section 1: Multiple Choice

1. The tone of the sentence is primarily:
    a. Factual
    b. Satirical
    c. Humorous
    d. Dreary

2. The purpose of the sentence is likely:
    a. Introducing characters
    b. Creating a setting
    c. Introducing a theme
    d. Establishing background

Section 2: Essay Question

In a short essay, describe the author's purpose in opening the novel *Pride and Prejudice* with the sentence found in the reading passage.

Figure 2.5: Sample test questions.

When teachers give students a sense of the close reading process (how to conduct it and its value), students are set up for success as they begin using it in class and on their own. Once they are familiar with the process and have seen the teacher model it, students can start to use it more independently with prereading activities.

Prereading Activities

If students are to be effective close readers of a challenging text, they must access their own background knowledge and opinions on the subject. The purpose of prereading is to help students link what they already know or believe about the subject with the ideas they will encounter in the close reading. Effective prereading activities lead students to accomplish this in class and demonstrate some of the methods they might use when working on their own (in their personal reading or in a testing situation). The prereading strategy will be highly effective if it allows students to approach the close reading passage with a clear understanding of their own background knowledge on the topic and with some level of curiosity about what the passage will suggest. There are many effective means for accessing background knowledge and getting students ready to participate in the close reading process. Next, we explore the levels of prereading strategies.

Levels of Prereading Strategies

It is important to first decide what kind of prereading strategy fits best with the purpose of the close reading activity. This depends on two factors: (1) the status of students in their understanding and use of prereading as a strategy, and (2) the subject and difficulty of the text. If students are just learning the prereading step, teachers can guide readers. If students have become more independent in their prereading abilities, they can use activities that involve less teacher direction. Further, if the subject of the close reading text is similar to material students have already encountered in class, teachers might select more directive strategies in which the teacher will help students make specific connections to material already covered. If the close reading text is more generalized or does not specifically connect with previous content, teachers might have less need to direct students toward overt connections.

Two categories group strategies based on the amount of teacher direction needed: (1) teacher-led prereading strategies and (2) independent prereading strategies.

Teacher-Led Prereading Strategies

These activities will be useful when students are just learning the prereading step of the close reading process and when the teacher wishes to directly connect the close reading passage to content previously taught. These strategies include overt linkages, skimming, and teacher-prepared notes.

Overt Linkages

In the case where the close reading passage is relevant to previously covered content, teachers may wish to use overt linkages to directly connect the two to prepare students to read deeply (Marzano Research, 2016b). Establishing these linkages can be as simple as suggesting students keep in mind prior learning as they read. If the prior learning is complex or if it has been some time since the teacher covered it, the teacher might be more specific in recalling the previously learned knowledge by using a class discussion or graphic organizer. Planning is essential and can be very straightforward.

An example might occur in an eighth-grade social studies class studying the documents associated with the American Revolution. If students have recently studied a short passage from Thomas Paine's 1776 book *Common Sense* and are now turning to a study of the Declaration of Independence, the teacher would want them to make the connection between the ideas presented in each document. In planning to share this linkage with students, the teacher might note the following.

- I will make connections between the documents, including an attack on the value of British rule over the American colonies, as well as the nature of government in a monarchy versus the nature of an independent United States.

- I can share this with students by asking them to reflect on what they learned in studying *Common Sense*, including Paine's claims that monarchy is sinful and unnatural.

- I will then ask students to look for ways in which Paine's ideas may have influenced the writers of the Declaration of Independence.

Skimming

Skimming is worthy of direct instruction as a reading and study skill. Students need the ability to quickly assess the subject and some specifics of nearly all their substantial reading, and most publishers design textbooks to support students' skimming the text before reading. Not all close reading passages are good candidates for skimming. When students skim, they look at section headings and subheadings to establish the content and attempt to summarize what they are about to read. If the passage does not have these structures or if the passage is quite short, it may not support skimming, so teachers should use this strategy judiciously.

When teachers structure a close reading passage to support skimming, providing students with a guide or worksheet can be very effective. The guide can be as robust or as simple as needed for the passage. Of course, students should already be familiar with the basics of skimming before using it with a close reading passage. When skimming, students should note the following (Marzano Research, 2016b).

- Headings

- Subheadings

- Topic sentences

- Bold, italicized, or repeated terms or phrases

Finally, students should summarize what they have skimmed and then generate questions about what they will read.

Teacher-Prepared Notes

While the ultimate goal of teaching the close reading process is for students to read and analyze a passage independently, beginning close readers will rely on teacher support. They need to build confidence that they can find what is important in the text, and teacher-prepared notes can be an effective way of doing this (Marzano Research, 2016b). While teacher-prepared notes are an important and powerful teaching tool, teachers should only use them in the earliest stages of teaching close reading.

Teacher-prepared notes usually outline the information in the passage. Additionally, the teacher's notes may call the students' attention to one or two key literary devices at work in the text, provide a specific example of a device, and then ask students to find and analyze other devices. Teachers distribute the notes before students encounter the passage, and the class discusses their expectations. Teachers can suggest students ask questions from the notes to promote the students' reliance on their notes as a structure for reading the text.

Independent Prereading Strategies

Independent prereading strategies may be more appropriate for students who have gained some familiarity and are building their level of confidence with the close reading process. In general, these strategies are more student centered and rely on students' ability to readily access background knowledge without much support from the teacher. Independent prereading strategies include informal hooks, What Do You Think You Know?, preview questions, and anticipation guides.

Informal Hooks

Informal hooks can be one of the most powerful and diverse methods of prereading (Marzano Research, 2016b). An *informal hook* is when the teacher designs and presents any form of media to the student to stimulate interest in the reading. Typically, the teacher will present this activity at the very beginning of the close reading period. It may take the form of presenting a painting or picture that accesses the subject or theme of the passage. Other possibilities include a short video clip, an audio clip (such as a song and the associated lyrics), newspaper headlines, a letter to the editor, or any other short, attention-grabbing media that will get students thinking about the subject of the passage.

To determine the media to present to students, the teacher starts by identifying the most interesting aspect of the content. Another method is for the teacher to consider the academic focus of the text and whether it might constitute something interesting to students. For example, a teacher dealing with a unit on mythology might introduce the notion of heroes by playing a short excerpt from a movie like *Clash of the Titans* to intrigue students about heroes. On the other hand, she might choose an appropriate satirical movie clip, such as an excerpt from *Monty Python and the Holy Grail*, to accomplish the same goal from another angle.

What Do You Think You Know?

The What Do You Think You Know? strategy is especially effective if students are likely to approach a passage with strong opinions or preconceived notions about the subject. In this strategy, teachers simply ask students what they think they know about the upcoming topic (Marzano Research, 2016b). Each student creates his or her own list of ideas and opinions, and the teacher then asks students to pair up and discuss their previous knowledge and ideas. The paired students create a combined list of their most original or most important ideas. Then, the class comes together and pairs share their lists with the rest of the class. The teacher creates a whole-class list of what students already know about the content. This list and the students' own experiences in accessing their existing opinions form a good starting point for encountering what an author may say on the subject. Students can then see where the list validates their ideas and where the author's ideas differ.

Preview Questions

Preview questions comprise a tried-and-true method of accessing background knowledge and opinions prior to reading the passage (Marzano Research, 2016b). This strategy is very effective, but teachers should avoid overusing it when preparing students to read a text.

To use the preview questions strategy, the teacher asks students questions related to the passage they will close read in order to access their prior knowledge and generate curiosity. These questions provide students with clues about what is important in the passage and foster greater engagement with the text. Teachers should carefully choose a small number of questions. They should access background knowledge in a general way but not give away the specifics of the author's position on the subject. For example, if the close reading passage is from the opening scene of *Romeo and Juliet* (Shakespeare, 1595/1997b), the preview question might be, Which is more important, sticking up for yourself or following the rules? The teacher would direct students to answer the question individually first, then pair up to share and discuss their responses. Finally, the teacher would conduct a class discussion of the question.

It is important to note that the teacher must clearly understand the theme of the passage to generate preview questions. The preview questions must reach the heart of the issue at hand but must never give away what will happen in the passage.

Anticipation Guides

Anticipation guides are effective with both beginning and more experienced close readers, so teachers can also adapt them to serve as a teacher-led previewing strategy (Marzano Research, 2016b). An *anticipation guide* is a series of statements about the passage. Usually, students respond to the statements with their own opinions on the topic. Further, they will encounter differing opinions from other students' responses to the same statements. Students can then develop their own questions as the basis for their reading.

Teachers must carefully plan an anticipation guide. Not only does the teacher need to develop statements about the topic but also anticipate the questions such statements may generate. Anticipation guide statements closely resemble preview questions; they are just statements rather than questions. The statements can probe more deeply into students' opinions and thoughts. For example, if the class is about to read a scene from *Romeo and Juliet* (Shakespeare, 1595/1997b), the teacher might present statements that access the action of the scene but do not refer to the specifics of the play, as the following figure 2.6 exemplifies.

Consider the following actions and related social attitudes. Rank the actions in order of seriousness, with the most serious at the top.

- Killing someone for revenge

- Killing someone by mistake when fighting

- Picking a fight

- Killing someone in self-defense

Figure 2.6: A sample of anticipation guide statements.

Each of these actions occurs during act 3, scene 1 of the play. Students will think carefully about the subtle differences between the descriptions of these actions and provide strong opinions of their own positions. This will increase their engagement with the actions and opinions of the characters as they close read the scene.

Choosing the right prereading activity for students depends both on the text students will read and on their close reading ability.

The Right Prereading Activity for Students

As stated previously, teacher-led strategies are best for beginning close readers, and independent strategies support more experienced close readers. The activities in the preceding sections are just a few suggestions; there are many alternative prereading activities, and teachers who keep the overall abilities of their students firmly in mind will choose what is best for them.

When making a match between the prereading activity and the text, teachers should consider several factors. These include the skill the close reading passage addresses, the subject of the passage, the level of challenge the passage will present to students, and, possibly, the genre of the passage.

Teachers often choose a close reading passage because it features a literary or figurative device that students are learning to analyze. In this case, the prereading activity should center around instruction on that device. Usually students have already had direct instruction on the device, and the close reading passage presents the opportunity for students to practice and deepen their analytical abilities with that device. The prereading activity should refresh students' memories of the device's fundamental elements and may provide an example or two as a prompt for students to explore the text. In a case like this, overt linkages are appropriate.

When a teacher selects a close reading passage because of theme—with the focus less on a specific literary device and more on the subject and overall effect of the passage—a more generalized prereading activity works best. In this case, students need to be thinking about opinions and background knowledge specific to the subject. Teachers would likely choose to do an anticipation guide or a preview question.

If a close reading passage will clearly present a challenge to the students' current close reading abilities, it is often best for teachers to present students with a prereading activity that narrows student focus to selected literary devices or one part of the subject. A truly challenging passage can overwhelm students, so narrowing the focus to one part of the text helps them experience success. Here, a teacher might use teacher-prepared notes or overt linkages.

Finally, the genre of the passage may affect the teacher's selection of prereading activity. Prose fiction is often straightforward for students, as is informational text. Drama and poetry, on the other hand, have structural elements that may put students out of their comfort zone. A change of genre may even challenge students who have become adept at close reading prose. It may be that a teacher chooses to use a teacher-led strategy when she first approaches drama or poetry, even if her students have been successful with independent strategies when reading prose.

Summary

In this chapter, we identified four important considerations when teachers select a passage for close reading. These include (1) the level of both student and teacher interest, (2) the level of complexity, (3) the type of text (informational or literary), and (4) the length and purpose of the passage. Teachers then need to prepare to teach the passage with their own careful close reading of it. Additionally, teachers should introduce students to the close reading process before they ask students to execute it. Teachers should model the steps to help familiarize their students with the process. Finally, teachers should consider two levels of prereading strategies when selecting an appropriate activity for the passage.

Chapter 2: Comprehension Questions

1. What are some important considerations when choosing a passage for close reading?

2. What important steps should a teacher take in preparing to teach a close reading passage?

3. What is the difference between teacher-led and independent prereading strategies?

4. Describe four considerations for selecting the most appropriate prereading activity.

Chapter 3

READING TWICE AND ANNOTATING

Once students complete an appropriate prereading activity, the next step is for them to read the passage twice and annotate it. The purpose of this step is twofold: (1) for students to encounter the text for the first time, and (2) for them to read actively, looking for aspects of the text they wish to explore more deeply. Obviously, students don't come to this activity accomplished in the skill of reading and annotating; teachers must directly teach it to them. As with any skill, practice deepens students' abilities and provides increasing assurance that they have the knowledge and ability to perform it well.

In this chapter, we look closely at how teachers can raise student awareness of what and how to annotate. Central to this process is understanding the literary techniques authors use in their writing. We will briefly discuss the kind of techniques students should focus on when reading and annotating.

Reading a Passage

At this step, students will read the passage twice. This encourages students to do more than read for understanding (which they can usually accomplish with one quick read-through). Rather, the purpose of close reading is a deeper appreciation of what the author is doing in the text and how he or she is doing it. Next, we consider the first reading and second reading in more depth.

First Reading

In the first reading, beginning students will focus on understanding, and there is nothing wrong with this. Once students are familiar and accomplished with the close reading process, they will be able to look for devices, ideas, and those moments when their minds signal that something interests them. They will learn to use those moments for annotation, but even beginning close readers can focus on surprises in the text—whether plot elements in a literary text or big ideas in an informational text.

When learning how to do this first reading, most students will benefit from watching their teacher model the process. It is often a good idea for teachers to use an audiovisual method to demonstrate the process. Ideally, teachers will use a method in which they can write directly on the text, as students will most commonly close read printed texts where the reader can write directly on the passage. One option is for the teacher to project the passage on an interactive whiteboard—so he or she can actively mark up the passage or add comments, also modeling some of the steps of annotation. A document camera can offer the same possibilities. If these options are unavailable, an old-fashioned overhead projector and a transparency of the passage accomplishes the same task.

As an example of modeling a first reading, consider this informational passage (the second paragraph of the Declaration of Independence) that might be taught in eighth or ninth grade:

> We hold these truths to be self-evident, that all men are created equal, that they are endowed by their Creator with certain unalienable Rights, that among these are Life, Liberty and the pursuit of Happiness.—That to secure these rights, Governments are instituted among Men, deriving their just powers from the consent of the governed, —That whenever any Form of Government becomes destructive of these ends, it is the Right of the People to alter or to abolish it, and to institute new Government, laying its foundation on such principles and organizing its powers in such form, as to them shall seem most likely to effect their Safety and Happiness. Prudence, indeed, will dictate that Governments long established should not be changed for light and transient causes; and accordingly all experience hath shewn, that mankind are more disposed to suffer, while evils are sufferable, than to right themselves by abolishing the forms to which they are accustomed. But when a long train of abuses and usurpations, pursuing invariably the same Object evinces a design to reduce them under absolute Despotism, it is their right, it is their duty, to throw off such Government, and to provide new Guards for their future security.—Such has been the patient sufferance of these Colonies; and such is now the necessity which constrains them to alter their former Systems of Government. The history of the present King of Great Britain is a history of repeated injuries and usurpations, all having in direct object the establishment of an absolute Tyranny over these States. (United States, 1776, para. 2)

Assume the class prepared to read this passage by doing a prereading activity such as overt linkages or an anticipation guide. While students almost certainly know about the Declaration, the simple fact is that most people rarely read the Declaration, so students may not know what the document actually says. Thus, the teacher should not assume students bring much preexisting knowledge to the passage. Further, a document crafted in 1776 brings many issues regarding vocabulary and style. These issues could be the focus of close reading, but for this example, assume the teacher wants students' to focus on the ideas and arguments presented in the passage. As such, the teacher might ease students' cognitive load by presenting them with definitions of terms that will likely challenge them as they first read, such as the following.

- **Endowed:** Provided with something by someone

- **Inalienable:** Something that cannot be taken or given away

- **Instituted:** Put in place

- **Deriving:** Coming from

- **Prudence:** Good judgment

- **Transient:** Only for a short time

- **Shewn:** Old form of *shown*

- **Usurpations:** Forcefully taking someone's power or property

- **Evinces:** Indicates or shows

- **Despotism:** Ruling with total power

There are many other candidates for this list in the passage, so it could be extended. It may be, however, that some unfamiliar words should remain unfamiliar as a potential topic for discussion. One candidate that might fall into that category is the term *self-evident*. Eighth- or ninth-grade students might struggle to understand the term, yet its meaning is central to the opening of the paragraph and including it in the discussion will introduce the importance of the meaning of the opening sentence. Teachers can make decisions about whether they provide all or some of the information students will need to understand the passage on first reading based on what they wish the reading to accomplish.

The teacher would then display the passage and model the first reading process. Figure 3.1 shows how the conversation might proceed.

In skimming the passage, I can see that a few words sound familiar; I will want to think about my past understanding as I read.

Here's a word I might not know. I'd highlight it, so that I can look it up.

That sounds familiar, and I agree.

I've heard that before, but maybe I didn't know that the Declaration says they come from the Creator and can't be taken away.

I have no idea why this section is between dashes. Is that important? I should note it as something to think more about.

We hold these truths to be self-evident, that all men are created equal, that they are endowed by their Creator with certain unalienable Rights, that among these are Life, Liberty and the pursuit of Happiness.—That to secure these rights, Governments are instituted among Men, deriving their just powers from the consent of the governed, —That whenever any Form of Government becomes destructive of these ends, it is the Right of the People to alter or to abolish it, and to institute new Government, laying its foundation on such principles and organizing its powers in such form, as to them shall seem most likely to effect their Safety and Happiness. Prudence, indeed, will dictate that Governments long established should not be changed for light and transient causes; and accordingly all experience hath shewn, that mankind are more disposed to suffer, while evils are sufferable, than to right themselves by abolishing the forms to which they are accustomed. But when a long train of abuses and usurpations, pursuing invariably the same Object evinces a design to reduce them under absolute Despotism, it is their right, it is their duty, to throw off such Government, and to provide new Guards for their future security.—Such has been the patient sufferance of these Colonies; and such is now the necessity which constrains them to alter their former Systems of Government. The history of the present King of Great Britain is a history of repeated injuries and usurpations, all having in direct object the establishment of an absolute Tyranny over these States.

Sounds like a grammar error.

That is a really long sentence that just ended, and I'm not sure I understand it. I got lost in trying to follow it as I read. When I read the second time, I want to stop here and see if I can put the meaning together.

Another long sentence. Another place to revisit to because I don't get it now.

The conjunctions but and yet are signal words. I will look for a shift in meaning or ideas.

I just noticed how many words are capitalized that I didn't expect to be capitalized.

At the end of the first reading, I understand that the colonies don't like the British government and the king, and they are saying that the British are taking away their rights, rights they claim come from the Creator and cannot be taken away. The section in the middle was hard to understand, and I don't quite get it on the first reading, so that might be something to focus on in the second reading. I also saw lots of complicated and different writing issues (like the capitalization and the dashes) that I need to think about.

Source: United States, 1776, para. 2.

Figure 3.1: First reading annotation modeling.

Keep in mind that the teacher models the thought processes of an experienced close reader—students should not expect or be expected to think independently at the same level. If the idea of processing while reading overwhelms students, the teacher might simply encourage them to read the passage without any processing the first time (in effect, adding a third reading at the front end), and then look to reason in the next reading. Eventually, students should be encouraged to think carefully during that first reading. The comment at the end of the example (see figure 3.1, page 43) indicates the level of thought students might be expected to achieve after the first reading once they have learned the process well. Summarizing one's overall thoughts after the first reading will provide a good basis for the second reading. Modeling that behavior demonstrates the kind of thinking the teacher wishes students to display after the first reading. Students might also informally come up with questions they want to pay more attention to during the second reading, such as the following four.

1. What does the middle portion of the passage mean?

2. Why are the sentences in the middle portion so difficult?

3. Why does the author capitalize certain words?

4. Why does the author use dashes?

With this preparation, students can proceed to the second reading and annotate the passage as they go.

Before we move to the second reading, consider the common situation in which students do their first reading and find very little. This happens at all grade levels and levels of close reading experience—not just with beginners. In this situation, teachers must encourage students to be resilient. Further, they must be encouraged to continue to revisit the passage with determination.

One way teachers can help struggling (or beginning) close readers is to provide them with a list of things to look for as they read the first time. This could be modified forms of the checklists for teachers (see figures 2.2 and 2.3, pages 26–27). Teachers can also refer to the list of literary rhetorical devices later in this chapter (see Using Literary and Rhetorical Devices, page 50) for possible tools for students. Ideally, teachers can craft the guide to focus on the particular aspects of the text the teacher wishes students to see, though students should still be open to finding anything valid in the passage. Another method is for teachers to ask students to identify moments in the passage where they are confused or surprised. It is often at these points that discussion can open up between students, first to share their frustration with the passage, but then to break through into something the class can discuss. Other methods include the following examples.

- For beginning students, a quick conversation with peers will often draw out at least one thing to look for in the second reading. If that fails, a class discussion may be effective.

- Once students have some background in close reading, encourage them to start simply. Often students are looking for something very deep and not finding it. Saying the obvious and thinking about it a bit will often spark something deeper.

- If the first and second readings produce nothing, try a third or fourth. If necessary, go back to modeling a reading with students and draw out one or two things for the next reading.

- Assure students that there is something to notice; it is not a random passage that may, in fact, have nothing to notice. The passage was chosen for a reason, and their job is to find out why. This is an essential point to make in preparing students to engage with texts on standardized tests. They need the resilience to continue when their first encounters seem fruitless.

Keep in mind that the purpose is to encourage students to be able to find a way into the text by themselves, rather than the teacher pointing the way. The American poet Walt Whitman (1991) had fine advice for the readers of his poetry as they struggled to discover what he was placing there, and it remains fine advice for close readers: "Failing to fetch me at first, keep encouraged, / Missing me one place, search another, / I stop somewhere waiting for you" (p. 79).

Second Reading

The second time through the passage is a slightly more task-focused reading. Based on the evidence found in the first reading, in the second reading students look for more reactions and information that support answers to their questions. However, they should always remain open to a new insight; sometimes just reading the same material a second time will spark something new.

In modeling the second reading for students, teachers must reinforce the power of active reading based on their initial observations. Once again, here are the four questions students might have wondered about on the first reading of the passage from the Declaration of Independence.

1. What does the middle portion of the passage mean?

2. Why are the sentences in the middle portion so difficult?

3. Why does the author capitalize certain words?

4. Why does the author use dashes?

As the teacher models the second reading, she might prepare students for understanding the process with the following comments.

> As I get ready to read the passage a second time, I start by reviewing and thinking about my four questions. Given those questions, it is clear that the middle portion of the passage is a place I really need to look at. Also, I have two questions about the mechanics of the passage. Those may be harder to answer with a second reading, but I want to pay attention to whether I have any ideas about the dashes and capitalization as I read. At the same time I am doing all this, I want to be open to new ideas. Wow, that is a lot to focus on! That means I'll probably need to read the second time at a slower pace than the first time.

Teachers should send the message that method is their first concern. After all, close reading is a process, and the step details are important. The class returns to the passage, perhaps using a new copy of the passage for the second reading. This isn't always necessary, but in teaching students to do the second reading sometimes it is a good idea to remove the initial comments for clarity. Once students can accomplish the process on their own, they can annotate the text next to their annotations from the first reading. Figure 3.2 (page 46) shows model annotations for the second reading.

Once the teacher has walked students through this portion of the reading, it can be useful to place the questions from the first reading next to the ideas that come from the second reading (see figure 3.3, page 47). It may well be that their second reading ideas do not represent complete answers to their questions—but at this stage, that's OK. Ideally, after the second reading students will generate questions for a final, true close analytical reading of the text.

A comparison such as the one in figure 3.3 will demonstrate to students that the process is working, even though the answers at this point do not constitute a true close reading of the passage. As students learn the reading twice and annotating step, it will quickly become important for them to know something about the annotation process. In the following section, we consider how to develop this skill with students, guiding them toward a sense of what they should annotate and what to ignore.

All the capitalized words are nouns. Maybe that is the pattern.

This long sentence keeps adding deeper ideas on the same topic, why a form of government should be changed. That is a central idea so maybe that's why the sentence is so long. This idea needs lots of support.

Both dashes are followed by the word That and then what follows tells more about what came before. So the dash could signal something important to follow.

This sentence is still hard to understand, but having thought about the sentence before, it looks like this sentence gives another reason why things should be changed. People have the right to a government that they are comfortable with.

Here's a dash again, and what follows gives more information about what came before, just like the pattern above.

We hold these truths to be self-evident, that all men are created equal, that they are endowed by their Creator with certain unalienable Rights, that among these are Life, Liberty and the pursuit of Happiness.—That to secure these rights, Governments are instituted among Men, deriving their just powers from the consent of the governed, —That whenever any Form of Government becomes destructive of these ends, it is the Right of the People to alter or to abolish it, and to institute new Government, laying its foundation on such principles and organizing its powers in such form, as to them shall seem most likely to effect their Safety and Happiness. Prudence, indeed, will dictate that Governments long established should not be changed for light and transient causes; and accordingly all experience hath shewn, that mankind are more disposed to suffer, while evils are sufferable, than to right themselves by abolishing the forms to which they are accustomed. But when a long train of abuses and usurpations, pursuing invariably the same Object evinces a design to reduce them under absolute Despotism, it is their right, it is their duty, to throw off such Government, and to provide new Guards for their future security.—Such has been the patient sufferance of these Colonies; and such is now the necessity which constrains them to alter their former Systems of Government. The history of the present King of Great Britain is a history of repeated injuries and usurpations, all having in direct object the establishment of an absolute Tyranny over these States.

It looks like the pattern of the passage is that it goes from general ideas to specific. From reasons why any people can change any government to the Colonies wanting to change their government.

Source: United States, 1776, para. 2.

Figure 3.2: Second reading annotation modeling.

Annotation Skills

Few students truly know how to annotate well; the result is often pages nearly fully highlighted in yellow. It is vital that teachers directly teach and model (live, on an overhead projector or a computer screen with a projector) the annotation process using the method discussed in this chapter. While we modeled the steps to students before, it is now time to break the steps down into specific decisions they will make as they close read, and then help them to develop the skills of making such decisions. Otherwise, students are likely to annotate either everything or almost nothing, making this step of little value.

First Reading: Questions	Second Reading: Ideas
What does the middle portion of the passage mean?	At this point, it appears the author is giving deeper and deeper support to the idea that governments can and should be changed.
Why are the sentences in the middle portion so difficult?	The language is challenging, but because the ideas go deeper and deeper, the sentences get longer and longer and are harder to follow.
Why does the author capitalize certain words?	It appears that the capitalized words are nouns. Was it common practice at the time to capitalize nouns?
Why does the author use dashes?	At this point, the pattern seems to be that more information about the preceding idea follows the dashes.

Figure 3.3: Organizing questions and ideas.

If a student is to annotate a text, the teacher must provide the text in a form which *can* be annotated. While technology is making advances in this realm, many applications that allow textual markup can be cumbersome and frustrating to use. Simply circling in pencil and a quick word or two in the margin is much more efficient. Encourage students to work with a printed text and traditional annotation tools—a highlighter, a pencil, or a pen.

As with any form of procedural knowledge or skill, people develop their process in steps and over time. A simple set of steps for annotations might be as follows.

1. Determine that something is a candidate for annotation.

2. Annotate in some fashion.

3. Comment on the annotation.

In the following sections, we will explore these steps in more detail.

Determine That Something Is a Candidate for Annotation

Central to successful annotation is the decision about what is important and a candidate for annotation. The sense of what is vital develops over time and is directly related to developing students' abilities to pay attention to their internal reactions to a text. Teacher modeling (as described on page 65) will help students understand the process of sorting through everything to find something worth noting. This doesn't come easily; it takes a lot of practice, and students need to be patient with themselves. Some potential criteria that would nominate a piece of text as a candidate for annotation might include the following.

- A short passage, sentence, or phrase that seems significant in the context of the reader's focus for reading the text

- A piece of text that resonates with something the author has been emphasizing in the passage

- Something in the text that generates a question in the mind of the reader or that presents something puzzling

- A piece of text that appears to be an example of a rhetorical or literary device important in the context of the passage

Obviously, this list is only a start and many other potential criteria could work. Each item needs thorough explanation, with clear examples and nonexamples, as well as careful and consistent modeling and practice.

Returning to the Declaration of Independence example in figure 3.2, look carefully at the annotation choices in the opening portion of the first sentence: "<u>We</u> hold these truths to be <u>self-evident</u>, that <u>all men are created equal</u>, that they are endowed by their Creator with certain unalienable Rights, that among these are <u>Life, Liberty and the pursuit of Happiness</u>" (United States, 1776, para. 2).

Here, the annotated text is underlined; in class, students might use a highlighter.

In this example, the teacher annotates *We* simply out of a resonance with something familiar; perhaps the reader has heard this word before in connection with the Declaration of Independence. In that sense, the teacher annotates the word simply because something in his or her past suggests it is important and thus something that generates a question in the mind of the reader or presents something puzzling. In fact, it is vitally important to understanding the impact of the document because the plural first person implies a collective that suggests a group—a group of political figures setting out to start a new nation. Students might not make this connection, but responding to past information is a valid way of interacting with the text. The reader annotates it because it seems important.

The teacher annotates *self-evident* for a different reason: it is an unknown word, so students should note it and then explore it later. Once again, this text is annotated because it represents a question in the mind of the reader. Reading a text with a dictionary at hand is a good idea if students know how to use a dictionary properly in this situation. Their dictionary skills must be developed enough that they know not to simply accept the first meaning listed but to examine the possible meanings in context. Practice in class with good modeling will support the development of that skill.

Life, Liberty and the pursuit of Happiness also falls into the category of familiar words. Again, the reader annotates it because his or her brain signals that it's important. In a less-familiar text, this kind of annotation will happen less frequently, but teachers need to reinforce with students that they must develop a sensitivity to their own reactions. Sometimes this will cause students to annotate unimportant things. This happens often when students are learning the process, but eventually they become more adept at sorting through what is and isn't important.

Annotate in Some Fashion

Here, the reader actually marks up the text using a variety of tools—highlighters, colored pens or pencils, circles, brackets, and so on. Students can develop their own preferred method, but when they are just learning, the teacher should recommend, model, and consistently implement one method. One such method is for students to use different colored highlighters for different types of annotations. In the following example from the Declaration of Independence passage (see figure 3.4), a double underline indicates something important to the meaning of the text, a dashed underline indicates something rhetorically important, and a single underline indicates something quotable.

Comment on the Annotation

However, simply highlighting text is not annotating. It is important for students to process what they are annotating by remarking on the potential significance of the text or idea and possibly generating a question about it. Obviously, this requires thorough instruction and modeling, as commentary in the reading examples in the previous section shows (see pages 43–46).

We hold these truths to be self-evident, that all men are created equal, that they are endowed by their Creator with certain unalienable Rights, that among these are Life, Liberty and the pursuit of Happiness.—That to secure these rights, Governments are instituted among Men, deriving their just powers from the consent of the governed,—That whenever any Form of Government becomes destructive of these ends, it is the Right of the People to alter or to abolish it, and to institute new Government, laying its foundation on such principles and organizing its powers in such form, as to them shall seem most likely to effect their Safety and Happiness. Prudence, indeed, will dictate that Governments long established should not be changed for light and transient causes; and accordingly all experience hath shewn, that mankind are more disposed to suffer, while evils are sufferable, than to right themselves by abolishing the forms to which they are accustomed. But when a long train of abuses and usurpations, pursuing invariably the same Object evinces a design to reduce them under absolute Despotism, it is their right, it is their duty, to throw off such Government, and to provide new Guards for their future security.—Such has been the patient sufferance of these Colonies; and such is now the necessity which constrains them to alter their former Systems of Government. The history of the present King of Great Britain is a history of repeated injuries and usurpations, all having in direct object the establishment of an absolute Tyranny over these States.

Source: United States, 1776, para. 2.

Figure 3.4: A sample annotation.

Sometimes students don't quite know why they have annotated something. In this case, encourage them to generate a question out of the annotation. In the example of the Declaration of Independence passage, the reader annotated several capitalized words but was unsure why the author capitalized them, even in the second reading. The commentary then shifts to a question: was it common practice at the time to capitalize nouns? A student cannot answer this question during the reading twice and annotating step, but it can lead to more research or a larger class discussion if the student generates and then shares the question.

The following sections present some of the most essential literary and rhetorical devices, the ones most important to reading twice and annotating a text, but this list is incomplete. There are hundreds of devices, but teachers never teach most to secondary students. Teachers can equip students to continue to improve their skills throughout school and life by focusing on some of these key devices they will encounter.

Using Literary and Rhetorical Text Devices

In the close reading process, students must delve deeply into a passage, looking for things the author is doing and reacting to those things. For students to have a nomenclature, indeed, a set of priorities to look for in close reading, they need to be familiar with the literary and rhetorical devices authors use to connect with their readers. A teacher might provide instruction on all these tools (or just some of them), ask students to discover which tools an author is using in a passage, or direct their attention to one or two specific tools. In all cases, however, teachers must directly teach students how an author uses these devices. They must learn not only how to identify when an author is using a device but also begin to formulate answers regarding why an author chooses and uses it.

It is once again important to reinforce the point that while state standards often define two different types of writing—informational and literary—the devices are, to a large extent, the same. The following sections do not divide the devices by category. Teachers can teach students about informational devices (such as *occasion*) along with literary devices (such as *setting*). Students benefit by seeing the connections across these two genres.

The six devices I discuss next are (1) plot, (2) setting, (3) occasion, (4) characterization, (5) figurative language, and (6) tone.

Plot

Conflict is central to all stories. Without it, there is no plot. In informational text, even text that seems to do nothing but provide information, one can identify conflict as controversy, the controversy generated by such simple choices as the selection of information, for example. Conflict is the onset of interest, either in a story or in an informational text. It is best expressed as something versus something else. Some examples include man versus self, man versus his environment, and so forth.

Once the student identifies conflict in a literary text, he or she can begin to trace plot development. Gustav Freytag's (1876) *Die Technik des Dramas* features the now-famous diagram that helps students identify the essential elements of plot development. Figure 3.5 shows a plot diagram.

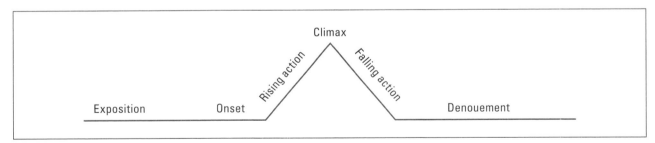

Figure 3.5: Plot diagram.

It is inherently limiting to reduce a literary text to a series of plot elements or apply a dramatic structural diagram to a full-length novel or epic. Focusing too much on the plot elements might obscure the unique elements that make a work worth reading. The plot analysis, however, represents an important starting point for students to more deeply analyze a complex text. The following are a few essential plot structure elements every student should know and be able to identify.

- **Exposition:** This is the introduction or background material that prepares the reader for the development of the central conflict to follow.

- **Onset:** This is the moment when the conflict becomes clearly present. In Freytag's diagram (figure 3.5), it is the moment when the plotline starts to move dramatically upward.

- **Rising action:** These are the many events that lead the reader to a deeper understanding of the developing conflict.

- **Climax:** This is the point when the conflict turns from development toward resolution. The climax can be difficult to determine; the reader really needs a retrospective view after finishing the entire work.

- **Falling action:** This is when the series of plot events moves toward resolution.

- **Denouement (or resolution):** This is when the conflict is resolved in some way or becomes unimportant to the immediate action of the story.

While informational texts do not have plots in the classic sense, they do have an organizational structure that mimics plot. The author establishes the conflict early by revealing the text's central argument. This argument may be very subtle. For example, in a social studies textbook, the presentation of a series of historical facts may appear to be nothing more than a presentation of history as information. Yet the author approached the presentation of these facts from a perspective and with a purpose in mind. He or she included some facts and omitted others. This essentially creates an argument in the text, one that students can identify and analyze if those students are sensitive to the choices an author makes. The rising action of an informational text consists of evidence the author presents in support of one or both sides of the argument. At some point, the author moves the text toward the conclusion he or she wishes the reader to adopt; the reader might consider this point the climax in an informational text. The falling action may be very brief, as it is often narrative text. A few comments that support the conclusion come fully at the end of the informational text, representing its resolution.

Setting

A deceptively simple device, *setting* has a powerful influence on the meaning and theme of any work. Most students can easily identify the setting of any literary text. However, it is much more difficult for students to answer questions such as, "What is the influence of the setting on the author's purpose, meaning, or theme?"

Setting is both the natural and artificial environment of any work. The *natural setting* of a work is its placement in nature (the time, location, or natural elements such as desert, mountains, city, and so on). The *artificial setting* of a work refers to the man-made elements present. The author may influence the setting in a dramatic work through the scenery, lighting, and other details. For example, consider the opening stage directions for Arthur Miller's (1949/2009) important play, *Death of a Salesman*:

> A melody is heard, played upon a flute. It is small and fine, telling of grass and trees and the horizon. The curtain rises. Before us is the Salesman's house. We are aware of towering, angular shapes behind it, surrounding it on all sides. Only the blue light of the sky falls upon the house and forestage; the surrounding area shows an angry glow of orange. As more light appears, we see a solid vault of apartment houses around the small, fragile-seeming home. An air of the dream clings to the place, a dream rising out of reality. The kitchen at center seems actual enough, for there is a kitchen table with three chairs, and a refrigerator. But no other fixtures are seen. At the back of the kitchen there is a draped entrance, which leads to the living-room. To the right of the kitchen, on a level raised two feet, is a bedroom furnished only with a brass bedstead and a straight chair. On a shelf over the bed a silver athletic trophy stands. A window opens onto the apartment house at the side. (p. 1449)

In this example, one can see the effects of the flute music, blue lighting, and detailed set description in establishing the artificial setting of the play.

It is in these spaces that the characters live, interact, make decisions, and move the story forward. Even in the world of fiction or narrative poetry, one can imagine the setting as a stage set, which includes anything that becomes important to the meaning and theme of the work through the characters' interaction with it. In addition to space, setting also involves time. The time of day, season of the year, the year itself, and so on all contribute to the setting and may impact the work's meaning and theme. The setting is the sum of the work's physical and temporal objects and artifacts.

Occasion

The informational text version of a setting, *occasion*, is equally influential. Every informational text has a specific occasion. The occasion of an informational text bears some similarities to the setting of a literary one. However, *occasion* suggests the setting of the writing, rather than the internal place and time of a narrative. Occasion includes elements such as time, physical location, and political, social, economic, theological, or philosophical background to the text. In considering the occasion, students may find two levels. First is the *immediate occasion*, which is an event or a situation that causes the writer to create a response. Second is the *larger occasion*, which is the subject's milieu—that set of opinions, emotions, and ideas that surround the subject. Sometimes these influences are plain; other times a careful understanding of the text and when the author wrote it lead to their discovery. There are also times when information about the occasion is unavailable to the reader. In these cases, and indeed with all texts, the text on the page is primary; occasion is secondary. With informational text, the reader may have the desire to see the text as a child of its occasion—its historical period, the social strife of the time, and so on. This reading may or may not be legitimate. If the reader cannot determine the effects of occasion on the writer—either from clear evidence in the text itself or from background information (such as a letter from the author discussing the occasion for the text)—assuming its influence is likely to result in an inaccurate analysis.

Characterization

Characterization is the method an author uses to introduce and develop the readers' understanding of a work's major characters. Characterization can be direct and indirect. *Direct characterization* is when the narrator (in fiction) or speaker (in poetry) makes statements about a character. Direct characterization tends to be rare in literature and creative writing; indirect characterization is much more common and subtler. *Indirect characterization* consists of a character's own statements and actions, as well as what other characters say or think about him or her. These can be difficult to separate from the rest of the narrative action.

Teachers can also group characters by type—including flat, round, static, or dynamic. A *flat character* usually represents one particular and not very developed attitude. A *round character* is the opposite—an attitude the writer fully realizes, representing multifaceted ideas. *Static characters* change very little or not at all across the entire work, while *dynamic characters* go through significant changes across the text.

When students think about a character in a work, a teacher might prompt them to ask themselves about the character's importance in the text and whether they can easily identify with the character or whether the character seems very different from them. Another important consideration for students is the character's judgment or decision making in important situations in the text. Finally, tracing a character's growth through the text is often a signal to the theme or main idea.

Figurative Language

Figurative language is the imaginative method of saying one thing and meaning more than that one thing. Figurative language involves an enormous number of related devices, and sometimes nomenclature can confuse teachers and students. Students will also encounter the term *rhetorical figures*, a broader term that includes figurative language. To speak figuratively is to step beyond the literal while keeping the literal fully in front of the reader. There are nearly countless figurative techniques, while this section covers just a few key devices. To introduce these devices, it is important to note that *comparison* is the cognitive tool around which figurative language revolves. The most basic devices of figurative language—simile, metaphor, and personification—all imply a comparison between inherently unlike things.

Simile and Metaphor

Both simile and metaphor involve comparing something literal with something unlike the literal, whether that thing is real or conceptual. In a *simile*, the author's comparison uses certain words or phrases (such as *like, as, seems, resembles, similar to, than*), while when an author uses a *metaphor*, he or she directly states the comparison, as if the literal *is* the figurative. For example, when Robert Burns (1794) wrote, "My love is like a red, red rose," he used a simile. When Shakespeare (1623/1997a) wrote, "All the world's a stage," he used a metaphor. Similes are relatively easy for students to identify since the key words are on the page (*like, as, seems*). Yet similes are so common in our language it is easy to overlook them. Metaphors, on the other hand, can truly challenge the reader, not only in discovering them but in understanding their structure.

In beginning to teach comparative devices such as simile and metaphor, a simple structure can help: "The author treats _____ as if it were _____." Such a simple sentence allows students to *unpack* a simile or metaphor in some depth by placing the literal in the first blank and the figurative in the second. Consider the example of Burns's (1794) simile, "My love is like a red, red rose." Plugging it into the sentence yields, "The author treats his love as if it were a red, red rose." From there, students can proceed with analysis.

A T-chart works well for this purpose, with the literal on the left side and the figurative on the right. Because the simile works through a detailed understanding of the figurative, students should analyze it first and then determine what the author implies about the literal. Figure 3.6 depicts how the chart might look after this first step.

Literal	Figurative
"My love"	"a red, red rose"
	Red Starts as closed bud then blossoms Has thorns Short life as beautiful, then dies Fragrant

Figure 3.6: Sample T-chart with qualities for figurative element.

There are many additional qualities of a red, red rose that might be listed on the right side (the figurative side) of the T-chart, and the more students list and then analyze these qualities, the deeper the reading of the simile will be. The second step is to take each quality on the figurative side and determine what the author implies about the literal by filling in the left side of the chart (see figure 3.7).

Literal	Figurative
"My love"	"a red, red rose"
Passionate Starts with potential, then develops into something more Potential of danger, sorrow Feels wonderful at first, may fade Delightful	Red Starts as closed bud, then blossoms Has thorns Short life as beautiful, then dies Fragrant

Figure 3.7: Sample T-chart for a simile.

In listing the implied qualities of the literal (love), the reader can see the power of the comparison in this simile. Far from being a simple comparison, the author implies a great number of specific qualities of his love in this one line of the poem. The poem continues to build on and deepen this comparison. By having students start with this simple analysis of the simile, students quickly develop a deeper close reading of the poem. Students can use the same process to unpack metaphors.

Personification

Personification is a figurative device that lends human qualities to animals, objects, or concepts. Again, it is built on the notion of comparison—some object, animal, or concept is the literal side of the T-chart and the figurative side is a human being or human quality. Thus, once the reader determines the aspects of humanity the writer is implying in the personification, he or she will be able to tell what the writer is implying about the literal side of the comparison. One of the most famous examples of personification is found in William Wordsworth's (1992) poem "I Wandered Lonely as a Cloud." In this poem, the speaker walks beside a lake and encounters a field of daffodils: "Beside the lake, beneath the trees, / Fluttering and dancing in the breeze" (Wordsworth, 1992, p. 44). Technically speaking, daffodils do not dance. That is something only humans do. But by assigning this human quality to the daffodils, Wordsworth establishes a clear image of the movement of the daffodils in the mind of the reader.

Students should be able to identify a writer's use of personification and discuss its effect—what is implied about the thing being personified and how that implication fits with the larger context of the work.

Tone

Tone refers to the author's attitude toward the subject, audience, or both. To be clear, tone is separate from mood. *Tone* is text evidence of the writer's attitude; *mood* consists of the emotions evoked in the reader by the text. Tone is useful in determining meaning and theme; mood is often so subjective it is not useful for the same task.

Tone is often the most powerful aspect of a text, whether literary or informational. Tone is also often the most challenging thing for students to learn to analyze well. Usually the author implies but does not directly state the tone, so unpacking these subtle implications is what makes it so incredibly difficult for students to master.

In discussing tone, consider the following five elements.

1. **Diction:** Word choice and the effects of denotation and connotation

2. **Imagery:** Language that invokes the senses

3. **Details:** Aspects that establish and maintain a tone

4. **Language:** Aspects of the use of language, such as figurative language, that affect the tone

5. **Syntax:** The structure of the writing that supports and maintains tone

To remember these elements, one can use the acronym DIDLS. See Scott and Newbold (2017) for more on DIDLS, including helpful infographics.

Additionally, it is important to note the tone pattern across a passage. In a short close reading passage, the tone may not change. However, one of the most effective writing techniques authors use is the *tonal shift*—an often-abrupt change in the tone of a passage for effect. To incorporate this aspect of tone, teachers can ask students to identify two tones. Those tone descriptors may be complementary if the tone is consistent, or contrasting if the tone shifts. When there is a tonal shift, the key analytical question then becomes, Why?

The following sections describe the five elements of tone in more detail.

Diction

Diction is about word choice. Not all words are important in analyzing tone; some choices have more impact than others. In teaching diction and helping students analyze the effects of word choice, teachers can start by identifying the differences between denotation and connotation. *Denotation* refers to the dictionary definition of a word. While the dictionary definition is important to identify, it usually doesn't have the effect that connotation does. However, especially when working with texts written prior to about 1950, it may be important to identify the dictionary definitions of words because meanings evolve over time.

Connotation refers to the emotional implications of a word. Choosing between words with the same denotations but different connotations is often an important technique writers use. The following simple example usually makes this clear to students: if I say that Josh is *childish*, it has a negative connotation, but if I say he is *childlike*, it carries a positive connotation (Arp & Johnson, 2009). Both words (*childish* and *childlike*) have essentially the same denotative meanings, but their connotations are different. In getting students to focus on denotative and connotative effects, the teacher can start by having them identify the words in a short passage that appear important—the *diction* words of the passage. These will be the words that have potential effects in the plotline.

Imagery

Imagery is a widely used and powerful literary element that involves the use of language that evokes the senses: taste, sight, touch, smell, and sound. Students are often taught about imagery in the elementary grades, so secondary teachers can usually build on their existing knowledge by asking them to look for a broader range of images. If students lack a solid foundation on the ideas of imagery or need a quick refresher, teachers can share examples of imagery that appeal to each of the senses, such as the following.

- **Visual:** *Dark trees with branches like hands loomed over the hikers.*

- **Auditory:** *The crowd roared with enthusiasm.*

- **Tactile:** *The ground was rough and cut his feet.*

- **Olfactory:** *Imagine the smell of fresh-baked chocolate-chip cookies.*

- **Gustatory:** *The crunch of the potato chips filled Sheena's mouth with a salty taste that brought her back to her childhood.*

Of course, as with diction, simply identifying the imagery is not enough; readers must focus on the *effect* the author is attempting to create by using the imagery.

Details

Details are the facts relevant to creating tone in the passage. They can be difficult to analyze because details are often thought of as the common objects of a setting or scene the author describes in a passage. Sometimes, however, details contribute to identifying the author's attitude toward his or her subject or audience.

Language

The author can use specific elements of language to establish tone. *Language* is a broad term, but in this context, it refers to the author's use of specialized language, such as formal language, slang, or jargon. *Formal language* engages all the correct uses of grammar and syntax and may include many words that derive from French, Greek, or Latin. Formal language can lend pomposity to a passage, or it may indicate something about the character's social class. *Slang language* may have just the opposite effect since it does not conform to the standard rules of grammar and usage. *Jargon* refers to words specific to an activity or profession. The author's use of jargon may cause the tone to be obscure to readers, except for those familiar with the activity. In addressing language, teachers should also ask students to consider the impact of figurative language on tone.

Syntax

The analysis of *syntax* refers to looking carefully at the grammatical structure of the language of the passage. This can be daunting for some students, often because their grammar knowledge may be limited. In its simplest form, readers discover syntax in language structure at the sentence level and then at the paragraph level, and this is usually sufficient for a close reading passage. At the sentence level, the reader should identify two things: (1) the overall pattern of the sentence structures and (2) when that pattern shifts. Writers will use syntactic shifts to signal readers to pay attention. For example, if a writer is being descriptive and presenting the reader with a series of complex, compound, and compound-complex sentences, he or she may suddenly include a short simple sentence. Readers should look closely at these shifts to see if something important is occurring.

Again, tone is a very challenging technique to analyze, and students struggle to be exact about it, even if they carefully analyze all the aspects. Teachers should encourage students to take a stab at the correct answer. If they come close, this is a starting point for a class discussion to help refine their ideas about tone and precisely identify it.

Theme

Theme is the point of a text—that message or idea around which the entire work revolves. Understanding the theme of the passage is the ultimate aim of interpretation. Because of its nature, identifying the theme is challenging for students. Too often, when asked what the theme of the passage is, a student will only respond with the topic: "It's about war," or "It's about a family." When students are trying to create a statement of the theme, it is useful to ask them to follow the formula, *topic + opinion*. Asking them to identify the author's opinion on the topic will push them closer to a true statement of theme.

The theme should state a generalization about the human condition. Keeping in mind that theme is the central organizing idea of the text, a theme should also imply the importance of the text. For a work, be it a novel, a play, or a poem, to remain on our intellectual radar past the few decades after its creation, it must promote a theme that is important, even profound. The more complicated the work, the more profound the statement of theme, and the more difficult it is to describe that theme in a single sentence.

Further challenging students is the fact that there is no one method for them to use to accurately determine a theme. The theme emerges, both out of a careful close reading of analytical methods the author employs and the attentive connection the reader maintains throughout the reading. That, of course, is a challenge for young readers, particularly when they engage with texts whose purpose is not primarily entertainment. Students need intellectual stamina to stay with a text, even though at times it may be far from engaging.

It is important to begin to think about theme early when interpreting a work. Readers should develop some ideas about theme at the middle stage of their analysis and keep their minds open to revising those ideas as their analysis becomes deeper and, hopefully, more profound. As students begin to make attempts at determining theme, they can look for evidence in the text itself. Occasionally, though rarely in literary works, the author or the author's persona in narration directly states the theme. More often, characters make statements that indicate to readers the direction to follow to discover the theme. These statements are often more obvious in a second or later reading of a text.

The Rhetorical Triangle

Every text, whether informational or literary, attempts to persuade readers in some way. Andrea A. Lunsford, John J. Ruszkiewicz, and Keith Walters's (2004) book *Everything's an Argument* makes this important point: nearly everything in this world—not just texts, but buildings, music, entertainment, sports, and so on—advocates a position on some topic and can be read as an argument. For example, why does a sports team select certain colors for its uniforms? Could those colors advocate for some connection to the location of the team, to values it might wish to espouse, and so forth? Thus, even though teachers use the following rhetorical techniques to engage with and analyze informational text, they really apply to both literary and informational text.

Aristotle defined the elements of rhetoric and the rhetorical triangle (rightly sometimes referred to as the *Aristotelian triangle*). The *rhetorical triangle* describes the relationship between the three basic elements in any argument: (1) the author or speaker, (2) the reader or audience, and (3) the subject (see figure 3.8, page 58). The triangle suggests an interactivity among all three elements, with each having an equal role to play in the argument in the text.

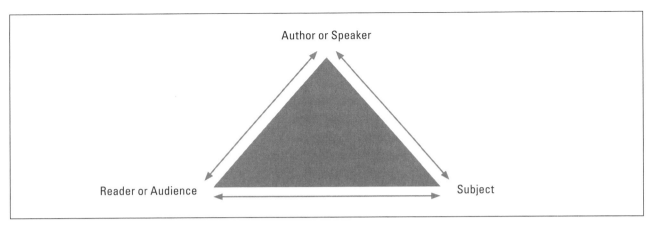

Figure 3.8: The rhetorical triangle.

Students have a proclivity to see the role of the speaker (or author of a written text) as authoritative. What the author intends in the text is primary; what the audience (the reader of a written text) thinks must be secondary, because it is not on the printed page. As described previously, the formalist approach would value the text itself over the author's intention or anything going on in the reader's mind. With the rhetorical triangle, Aristotle suggests an essential point: without the reader, there is no argument. Of equal measure in the argument's development is the subject. Both author and reader have relationships with the subject, and these are not the same.

The ways these three elements interact directly impacts the language and structure of the argument. It is important for teachers to open students' minds to the relationships among these three elements. The writer must choose a subject, and one consideration ought to be the potential interaction of the reader with that subject. Further, the reader makes a choice—to read or not to read—and one of his or her criteria will be the subject. The assumptions the writer makes about the audience will affect the rhetorical choices he or she makes when developing the argument. If the audience is highly educated on the subject, the argument can proceed assuming a certain level of audience understanding. However, if the reader has little background knowledge in the subject area, the writer will build a stronger argument when he or she does not assume that background knowledge.

Another issue to consider is the speaker in an informational text. Is the speaker the author? Encourage students to ask and carefully answer that question. Many writers create a persona that "speaks" in the text, and that persona may differ substantially from the author. Again, readers can only react to what is on the page; something a speaker says may or may not be the opinion of the author. Importantly, we cannot know. Students must be objective about evaluating the speaker and not assume the author and the speaker are the same.

Purpose

When an author sits down to write, he or she rarely begins to put words on the page without a specific purpose in mind. *Purpose* is the goal the writer has in mind as he or she writes. Once again, we should note that purpose applies to both literary and informational texts. As with *occasion*, determining purpose depends largely on the clues the writer provides in the text. It is important that students ask themselves about purpose. A useful question for readers to ask as they attempt to identify purpose is, "What did the writer want the audience to think or do as a result of reading this text?"

Purpose serves as the placemat, or background, of a text. In other words, everything that takes place in the text is because of the author's purpose. Consider the simile example from Burns's (1794) poem, "My love is like a red, red rose." What is Burns's purpose? One response would be to express his adoration for his love. Given that purpose, how does the simile fit into the purpose of the poem? It becomes one example, one literary device, one key idea that helps achieve Burns's purpose. Reading the entire poem might lead students to find many more examples of ideas and statements that help with the author's purpose.

To further clarify, consider the example of the paragraph from the Declaration of Independence (see page 42). The purpose of this document might be to state the reasons for the colonies declaring independence from Great Britain. Within the content of that purpose, the opening sentence, "We hold these truths to be self-evident, that all men are created equal, that they are endowed by their Creator with certain unalienable Rights, that among these are Life, Liberty and the pursuit of Happiness" (United States, 1776, para. 2), sets the stance for the entire argument that follows and supports the purpose of the document.

Elements of Argument

As described previously, any text making any kind of point is making an argument, and arguments are built around a structure. There are various models that describe the structure of arguments, such as Aristotelian and Rogerian; the structure for this book is based on the Toulmin model and consists of claims, grounds, backing, and qualifiers. Authors Katie Rogers and Julia A. Simms (2015) described these four elements of an argument as follows.

1. A *claim* is "a new idea or opinion. A claim may simply present information or suggest that certain action is needed" (p. 18).

2. *Grounds* refers to "the initial evidence—or reasoning—for a claim. Grounds are answers to the question, 'Why do you think your claim is true?'" (p. 18).

3. *Backing* is "information or facts about grounds that help establish their validity. In some cases, backing is simply a more in-depth discussion of the grounds" (p. 18).

4. *Qualifiers* refers to "exceptions to claims that indicate the degree of certainty for the claim" (p. 18).

It is important for students to develop an understanding of this basic structure throughout their school years. The book *Teaching Argumentation* (Rogers & Simms, 2015) covers the specifics about how teachers should introduce and develop students' ability to analyze these elements.

Students need to understand the basics of argumentation as a method for understanding how an author persuades his or her reader in a text. The ability to identify and evaluate the quality of arguments is essential to becoming a lifelong interpreter of written texts and a strong, reasoning citizen. These skills are so foundational to adult life it is possible to build an entire curriculum around them, and many state standards would support such a move. Even given a traditional approach to curricula, argumentation and the skill of analyzing arguments should make up a substantial portion of instruction. Close reading is one way teachers can incorporate these skills.

The Three Appeals

There are three methods the author may use to make his or her case to the audience. These methods are called "the three appeals" or *logos, ethos,* and *pathos* (according to Aristotle). They can apply to any text, informational or literary, though the descriptions below are confined to informational texts since they are commonly taught that way.

A *logos* appeal is an argument from facts and authority. The word *logos* is related to the word logic, and a logos appeal will offer a carefully constructed series of claims and supporting evidence that presents a clear, reasonable argument. Any reader who understands logic should be able to follow and agree with the argument. Typically, the evidence is solid and researchable. There may be a wide range of possible sources of evidence, including the opinions of experts in the field, commonly held beliefs of the society, and so forth. Students typically understand the structure of a logos argument since they are taught the basic tenets of it as they learn to write persuasive essays, which are essentially logos arguments.

An *ethos* appeal argues from the ethical position, an argument more in the world of *ought* than *is*. The writer of an ethos argument must first and foremost be credible, and it must be clear that for the field, he or she is an acknowledged expert. Also, the writer must support a position that is in the best interests of his or her audience. Ethos arguments may support the author's claims with evidence from commonly held values of the audience including, but not limited to, theological works, legal works, and so forth.

A *pathos* argument appeals to emotions. The author connects with the interests (and therefore the emotions) of his or her audience. The claims tug at emotions, not just pity and sympathy, but also pride, joy, patriotism, and the entire range of human feelings. It may appear the evidence is less solid at times in a pathos argument than in a logos argument, but it does not mean that a pathos argument is less valid or less effective. Emotions are powerful in persuasion.

When students are first introduced to the three appeals, teachers often present writing samples that exemplify one specific appeal. This is useful as students work to attain the concept of each appeal, but it should not suggest that writers pick one appeal and stick exclusively to that appeal throughout their text. Nor should readers look for a logos section of an argument and then a pathos section. The appeals work together, and some of the best arguments will access the power of all three appeals.

Summary

In this chapter, we explored the reading twice and annotating step of the close reading process. When students encounter a text for close reading, they should read it two times and annotate the text as they read. By the end of the first reading, students should identify some broad questions or ideas they plan to investigate more closely in the second reading. Effective annotation skills allow students to meaningfully mark up the text, rather than highlighting too much or not enough. Finally, knowledge of literary and rhetorical devices gives students a wide range of things to look for as they read twice and annotate a complex text. In the next chapter, we will discuss the generating questions and reading analytically steps of the process.

Chapter 3: Comprehension Questions

1. What are the differences in student actions between the first and second readings of the reading twice and annotating step of the close reading process?

2. What are some strategies to help students who find very little to annotate in their first and second readings of a close reading passage?

3. What criteria should students use to decide what to annotate as they read?

4. How should students use their knowledge and experience with rhetorical devices in the reading twice and annotating step of the close reading process?

Chapter 4

GENERATING QUESTIONS AND READING ANALYTICALLY

After reading twice and annotating, students move to the most important steps in the close reading process: generating questions and reading analytically. At this point, students have experienced the passage at least twice, connecting with their initial impressions of the text and annotating the text regarding those impressions. They will now further their conversation with the text by creating their own questions as they do a deep, close analytical reading of the passage. In this chapter, we will look at these steps in detail, with a focus on how to guide students to become more and more adept at creating and answering quality questions.

On the whole, these steps of the process are about developing students' ability to formulate good questions. As with other steps, teacher modeling of this process is essential. Students must approach the text with a mindset that close reading a text is different from simply reading the words for meaning. They must ask substantive questions. Further, they must develop the intellectual fortitude to ask lots of these questions and to be—temporarily at least—satisfied with not having the answers. The best way for teachers to make students aware of this mindset is to directly discuss it—the fact that this process represents a different kind of reading: active reading, reading with a questioning mind, and bringing one's own curiosity to the task. Rather than looking for the key events of the story so they understand what is happening, students need to look for the author's point or the purpose of the text. Rather than reading an informational text for information and to summarize, students should identify and evaluate the author's argument. Students will not develop these skills through independent silent reading; it takes direct classroom instruction and a caring but intensive teaching approach that supports development of the skills. Students might not immediately see the benefits, so teachers will need tenacity and patience as they learn.

The questions students ask are the key to their understanding a text. For those questions to be of high quality, students need to actively engage with the text (also see the discussion of analytical reading on page 67).

Student Questions

In the reading twice and annotating stage of the close reading process, students have their first opportunity to react to the text and formulate questions they will actively pursue as they do a deep analytical reading of the passage. Teachers should scaffold the text students encounter in the prereading stage and flesh out its meaning during the reading twice and annotating step. As students use that experience to generate close reading questions during this step, they should focus carefully on their own personal encounter with the text.

There are a number of characteristics that constitute a high-quality analytical reading question. Ideally, these questions result from a student's conversation with the passage, in something he or she has noticed and wishes to pursue. Further, such questions should be grounded in good rhetorical technique; in other words, they ask something about the author's method and purpose in creating the passage. For that to happen, students need to know what to look for in the passage, as described in chapter 3 (page 41). Once again, the quality of students' questions depends on how well prepared they are, so teachers should consider students' understanding of the literary devices and ideas at work in the close reading passage. If these abilities need development, initial lessons on specific techniques will help. It may well be that specific techniques are the center of instruction prior to students' encounter with a specific passage because of its focus on those techniques. This is often the case in the early stages of teaching rhetorical analysis. As students move past these initial lessons, they will be able to identify and analyze specific rhetorical devices on their own.

Students will benefit a great deal from a group discussion of what they have noticed in the two annotated readings when learning the process for generating questions. By regularly participating in discussion of a community-read text, students learn the kinds of questions to ask. When in a testing situation or when asked to close read more independently, students will need to rely on extensive class discussion experience to effectively work their way through their own evidence. It also is a good idea to occasionally allow students to work on their own, even in a class situation, to practice a testing situation.

To start the discussion, have students share their findings after their two annotated readings. The class can look for commonalities as a starting place for next questions. Just as important, the class can identify the places where one student comes up with something clearly grounded in the text no one else saw. That is something to celebrate and pursue. This issue might become a question for everyone, or it could be something that one student wishes to pursue in the next stage. Both possibilities could work.

Students also need to know how to deepen their questions and seek information at increasingly deeper levels. Students need to edit and revise their questions with prompts and probing from the teacher. As elementary students learn how to encounter texts, it is quite normal for them to ask *what* questions: "What is the author doing here?" "What structure can we identify in the text at this point?" The answers are basic devices of literature: "He is introducing a metaphor." "She has shifted the setting." At upper grade levels, student questions should shift from *what* to *how* and *why*, questions that are significantly deeper than the thoughts students might have if they were reading simply for pleasure, to get the plot and details of the text. *How* and *why* questions demand a deeper analysis of the text. The following are examples of appropriate, deep questions that could be the focus of analytical reading.

- How does the author create a certain effect?

- Why does the author introduce this new character at this point in the story?

- Why does the author switch from a logos to a pathos appeal at this point in her argument?

- How does the author accomplish that switch of appeal?

- How does the author craft the language on the page to create that feeling of sadness?

The answers to these questions are not literal or easy, but a student who can analyze text at this level is one who will be a strong close reader.

If the purpose of creating questions is to establish a starting point for encountering the text, then a conversation around the level of these questions helps all students understand the value of going deeper. At the start of any school year, students need teacher modeling on shifting their questions about textual evidence. Students often arrive in a class reticent about sharing their own ideas. The teacher must create situations in which students feel safe about trying out their ideas. At the start of instruction, the teacher can spend some time modeling for students, showing them how to take a basic observation of a text and expand it into a real question that goes deeper. Students will likely need some teacher-guided practice on this so they can gain confidence that they are beginning to format deeper questions.

As with annotation skills, the teacher should model forming deeper questions on a very short passage (perhaps no more than three or four sentences of prose or a few lines of poetry) similar to those students will be expected to close read later. Here the teacher should model the read twice and annotate step of the close reading process, taking the time to discuss why some things are annotated and others are not, and connect these steps with the overall goal of close reading—to determine deeper meaning in the text. From this foundation, the teacher can model the process of looking through the annotated evidence and formulating questions.

Throughout this instruction, teachers should pause and let students process the ideas and their thinking as they make each annotation and decision. Teachers shouldn't expect students to be able to make the same kind of decisions a teacher would make after this instruction. What teachers can expect is for students to begin to understand the kind of thinking they will eventually apply as they do the process themselves. So, when asking students to share their ideas after an initial reading and annotation of the text, patience is essential. Students need to be patient with themselves to see how they can apply the analytical techniques as they begin to try to form their own deeper questions. Teachers must be patient as well and, if possible, find a way to show students how to take what might initially be very low-level analyses or questions and transform them into more profound, interesting, and challenging questions. The message to students should be, "You may not be there yet, but you're on the right track! So, share your ideas with me and your classmates, and together we'll help you develop them."

Eventually, students will gain independence and reliably share their ideas with others. An effective way to begin this conversation, especially early in the school year, is to have students share their ideas and evidence in groups. Frankly, there is safety in numbers, and students will be a little more likely to discuss their ideas if the audience is small.

Let's return to our passage from the Declaration of Independence. Figure 3.2 (page 46) shows an example of the annotations a teacher generated with students after reading this passage twice and questions that emerged from the student's initial encounter with the passage.

To move forward from the annotations and generate deeper questions that will form the basis for analysis, teachers can guide students with the following steps.

1. Put students in groups and allow them to share their thoughts.

2. Combine and edit questions.

3. Prepare students to read analytically for a specific question.

We will explore each of these steps in the following sections.

Put Students in Groups and Allow Them to Share Their Thoughts

At the end of the reading twice and annotating stage, students should have a substantial number of annotations to share with their peers. To continue with the Declaration of Independence example from figure 3.2 (page 46), recall the types of questions considered in previous steps.

- What does the middle portion of the passage mean?

- Why are the sentences in the middle portion so difficult?

- Why does the author capitalize certain words?

- Why does the author use dashes?

Now the task is to take the questioning to the next level. Students should consider all their annotated evidence and share as much as they can with their peers in small groups. The teacher should ask each group to come up with one question students are curious about for the next stage of reading. Assume the class, divided into small groups, generates the following questions.

- Is the passage an effective argument, and if so, why?

- What kind of audience would understand this passage, given the difficult words and sentence construction?

- Is there sufficient evidence in the passage to support the conclusion reached at the end?

- Is the strong diction effective in the passage?

- Why is this passage considered so important? Is it really that important other than for United States history?

These questions are general in nature; they do not focus on specific text details. They are typical of the questions students generate at first because they tend to see the passage at the macro rather than micro level. Though broad, these questions are a good starting point for developing good analytical questions.

Combine and Edit Questions

Once the groups generate questions, the teacher places each group's questions on the board and leads the class in combining and editing them to come up with one or two questions for the entire class. In considering the five questions the class came up with in our example, we might notice, for instance, that they all deal in some way with the subject of the passage. Though many focus on an aspect of the passage (such as evidence or diction), collectively, all the questions deal with the purpose of the passage, an argument. For that reason, the first question (Is the passage an effective argument, and if so, why?) might be an effective analytical reading question. In looking at the passage as an effective argument, the class will examine all the issues the other questions raise, including evidence, diction, audience, and the import of the argument beyond its historical moment. If the class identifies the first question as the analytical reading question, each group might wish to take on the aspect it identified with its original question. In general, if a group of students seems attached to its question and resistant to combining and editing with the rest of the class, little is lost if that group analyzes the text based on its original question while the rest of the class pursues the combined questions.

Prepare Students to Read Analytically for a Specific Question

Once the students choose or create a specific question for the focus of analytical reason, it is often useful for teachers to provide instruction or a reminder on the relevant literary and rhetorical devices. This sets up students for success as they approach the analysis stage. In our ongoing example, having identified the analytical reading question (Is the passage an effective argument, and if so, why?), the class will want to have a brief discussion that reminds them of the elements of a strong argument. If the class has received instruction on these elements before, the teacher can provide a quick reminder before they read. At this point, the teacher would remind them of the importance of claims, grounds, backing, and qualifiers, as well as the important background elements involving the purpose, occasion, and audience of the argument. With this review in place, students are now ready for the true close analytical reading of the passage.

Analytical Reading

With a student-generated analytical reading question in mind, it is time for everyone to return to the text once more. This final reading is the heart of the close reading process in the sense that the teacher has carefully prepared students, and now they will apply that preparation to a detailed analysis of the passage. This time, students read for specific answers to the specific question. Students should make further annotations during this reading, perhaps with a different color highlighter. It may be that the teacher wants students to focus on one element of style this time through, or students may be allowed to discover any literary or rhetorical devices that seem important. Here again, evidence is the key. Students need to work with the text on a micro level at this point, drilling down to individual sentences, phrases, and words. The evidence gained at this stage will be the most important of the whole process because it will support emerging responses to the questions the students generate themselves.

Teacher guidance, especially when students are just learning to engage in this step, is essential so they stay focused on the questions they generated. However, emerging independence is vital. In a standardized-testing situation, the students must exercise these steps quickly and accurately, so it cannot be overemphasized that, while students need modeling and guidance, they must eventually take on these steps independently.

It may appear that we are often revisiting the point of encouragement and support, but this is key to effective close reading. Close reading is difficult, and it is a challenge for emerging literary analysts to see when they are right and when they are wrong in their analysis of a text. Students need to understand that the standard cannot be absolute perfection at every moment. As they learn this, they will make errors; it happens to everyone. The important thing is what the students do with those mistakes. If such a mistake causes a student to be silent and avoid offering ideas for fear of failure, then everyone loses. If the community is supportive in that moment, and the student learns and is encouraged to keep trying, then everyone wins.

We now consider reading in response to questions (how it is different than reading at earlier stages of the close reading process) and judging the effectiveness of arguments.

Reading in Response to Questions

At this stage, the student will maintain a specific focus and look for evidence specific to the question. If the question is broad (for instance, as in the Declaration of Independence example), the student may find lots of evidence to consider. A narrow question may provide less evidence, but it may also make answering the analytical reading question easier. As beginning students work on this step of the process, the teacher can direct them to start with basic elements of the question. If the question is related to the tone of the passage, some beginning students might do well to just look for diction, while others focus on imagery, and so on. More experienced readers may need a quick reminder of the elements of tone, but they can move to looking for all the elements immediately. Again, it is important to be patient and encouraging with beginners, but to move as quickly as possible toward student independence in this step.

Returning to the passage from the Declaration of Independence, the analytical reading question is, Is the passage an effective argument, and if so, why? A logical first step for a close reader coming to the text with this question in mind is to identify the elements of argument at work in the passage. Again, the class would likely review the four elements of an argument: (1) claim, (2) grounds, (3) backing, and (4) qualifiers (Rogers & Simms, 2015; see also page 59 to remind yourself of the definitions of these elements). Figure 4.1 depicts what students might discover after reading through the passage again with an eye toward identifying these elements.

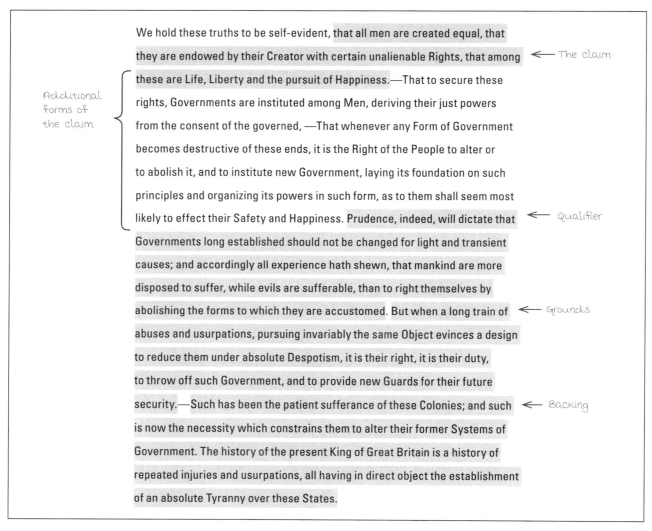

Source: United States, 1776, para. 2.

Figure 4.1: Analytical reading for argument structure.

In terms of the basic elements of an argument, this passage is exceptional in its structure. The reasoning here is substantial and well supported. Yet students might still struggle to see this, even when the structure is so clearly evident. Usually the reason for this lies in the challenge of the vocabulary and syntax of late–18th century language. Some students will identify major elements of the argument and a few may see all of them. After this careful analytical reading, the teacher should place students back in groups to compare what they have found. In sharing their annotations from the passage, students should quickly realize the profound structural nature of the argument in the passage. If they do not, it may be useful to take the entire class through the reasoning process of seeing that structure and then let the groups complete the work.

Judging the Effectiveness of Arguments

The analytical reading question asks whether the argument is effective, so the class must consider whether a well-structured argument means an effective argument. Similarly, if this is an effective argument, is structure the only way it is effective? We have reached the moment where the students and the teacher need the ability to analyze the elements of argumentation to see whether they are effective. Such strategies are important but are beyond the scope of this book. For information on this issue, the reader should consult *Teaching Argumentation: Activities and Games for the Classroom* (Rogers & Simms, 2015).

The teacher should return students to the passage and ask them to examine each element at a micro level, beginning with the Declaration of Independence's claim:

> We hold these truths to be self-evident, that all men are created equal, that they are endowed by their Creator with certain unalienable Rights, that among these are Life, Liberty and the pursuit of Happiness.—That to secure these rights, Governments are instituted among Men, deriving their just powers from the consent of the governed, —That whenever any Form of Government becomes destructive of these ends, it is the Right of the People to alter or to abolish it, and to institute new Government, laying its foundation on such principles and organizing its powers in such form, as to them shall seem most likely to effect their Safety and Happiness. (United States, 1776, para. 2)

Students may notice that the syntactical structure of the opening sentence is unique: "We hold these truths to be self-evident" suggests that a series of truths will follow, so the author is setting up the reader to watch for this list. Each item in the list begins with the word *that*. The author, in crafting this passage, chose to use parallel structure, where a series of words is repeated in the same structure, for effect. One implication of an author's use of parallel structure is to suggest to the reader that some form of comparison of the list items is important. The items may be of equal importance, or they may present a series of statements leading to a conclusion. To look at the specifics, it sometimes helps to take the list items out of the paragraph and turn them into a separate list like the following.

- That all men are created equal

- That they are endowed by their Creator with certain unalienable Rights

- That among these are Life, Liberty and the pursuit of Happiness

- That to secure these rights, Governments are instituted among Men, deriving their just powers from the consent of the governed

- That whenever any Form of Government becomes destructive of these ends, it is the Right of the People to alter or to abolish it, and to institute new Government, laying its foundation on such principles and organizing its powers in such form, as to them shall seem most likely to affect their Safety and Happiness

Examining the list in this manner makes it clear that the ideas build on one another. It is important to first establish that all men are created equal before claiming that their Creator endows them with certain inalienable rights and so forth. The payoff comes at the end of the claim, where the author states that those men have the right, in certain circumstances, to change the form of their government.

Once students establish the sequence of this rather long statement of claim, they easily see the power and effect of the list. Although the claim is complex, the author's logic is clear and builds slowly to the key idea of the passage, and indeed of the entire Declaration of Independence. There is already substantial evidence in the form of the sequence of quotations cited in the bullets above to prove the argument in this passage is effective.

What follows in the passage is a qualifier:

> Prudence, indeed, will dictate that Governments long established should not be changed for light and transient causes; and accordingly all experience hath shewn, that mankind are more disposed to suffer, while evils are sufferable, than to right themselves by abolishing the forms to which they are accustomed.

In this sentence, the author places *Prudence* at the start of the sentence. Close readers must ask, "Why?" It is certainly true that the author could have written the sentence differently with the same logical effect, so why place that word first? The answer is that this sentence follows the most important and most radical of the various claim elements—that people have the right to change their own government. By starting the next sentence with the word *Prudence* and then suggesting that wise men would think carefully about pursuing such a course of action as described in the previous claim, the author hopes to imply that these men are not acting rashly. With this qualifier, the author is addressing and attempting to defuse the strongest argument against the most radical claim—that it is a rash and poorly thought-out idea. At the end of the sentence (following the semicolon), the author also allows that humans typically suffer as long as they can tolerate it, rather than risk change. Thus, this qualifier sentence acknowledges a potential counterargument and works to establish the necessity of the claim.

The rest of the passage consists of grounds and backing:

> But when a long train of abuses and usurpations, pursuing invariably the same Object evinces a design to reduce them under absolute Despotism, it is their right, it is their duty, to throw off such Government, and to provide new Guards for their future security.—Such has been the patient sufferance of these Colonies; and such is now the necessity which constrains them to alter their former Systems of Government. The history of the present King of Great Britain is a history of repeated injuries and usurpations, all having in direct object the establishment of an absolute Tyranny over these States.

Note the next sentence begins with the word *But*, suggesting a shift in the argument. Students should pay special attention to words like *but*, *or*, *nor*, and *yet*, all of which signal shifts. The shift here is away from the qualifier in the previous sentence and toward the evidence that will support the claim. The evidence listed here is not specific, though the rest of the document (beyond our passage) will provide those specific instances. The grounds are general, as in "a long train of abuses." The backing is also general, as in "a history of repeated injuries and usurpations." Students may struggle to see this portion of the passage as effective, though the teacher can point them toward its purpose, which is to present the argument in general terms before more specific evidence is given later in the document.

Outside of its structure, students might note other evidence for or against the effectiveness of the argument. For example, in making strong diction choices such as *usurpations* and *Tyranny* in talking about the British government, and more specifically the English king, the author has effectively caught the attention of his audience: that very government and that very king.

At this point, the class has worked through the passage's specific evidence needed to make a judgment about the text's effectiveness as an argument. Students will be able to support their response to the analytical reading question with specific and detailed evidence. They will also want to address the issues raised in their other questions, subsumed under the question of the argument's effectiveness. Dealing with these questions at this point (when the argument is clearly defined), students will have greater insight into the reasons *why* the passage reads the way it does. Recall those other questions.

- What kind of audience would understand this passage, given the difficult words and sentence construction?

- Is there sufficient evidence in the passage to support the conclusion reached at the end?

- Is the strong diction effective in the passage?

- Why is this passage considered to be so important? Is it really that important other than for United States history?

With regard to audience, students would likely realize the primary audience for the passage is the British government, and specifically King George III. But the author intended a wider audience as well, justifying the actions of the new Americans before the entire world. The syntax and vocabulary indicate the author expected the audience to be educated and capable of careful reasoning. An interesting side conversation likely to emerge from this observation is whether the average American of the time would fully understand the document as it was publicly shared. That will lead to an examination of the level of education present in the American colonies in 1776.

Students would address the question of sufficient evidence in the examination of the passage as an argument, and they may have already noted that it is not specific enough (though the rest of the document solves that concern). They also had the opportunity to examine some of the diction in the passage as they discussed the argument question.

The final question is an important one to consider for two reasons. First, it clearly addresses the relevance of the Declaration of Independence on a broader stage than just that of American independence. This is a vitally important curricular issue, and the teacher should address it when students study the larger document. The second reason to consider this question is that it does not make a good analytical reading question because the details of the text lack grounds. This question addresses an issue beyond the text. It is an important issue, but students cannot address it by close reading. Such questions will arise as students examine passages, and teachers need to be aware of whether potential questions will provide strong analysis of the text or move the discussion beyond the text. Only questions grounded in textual evidence are good candidates for analytical reading questions. Extratextual questions are excellent potential discussion questions when students complete the close reading.

Summary

This chapter explored the steps at the heart of the close reading process: generating questions and reading analytically. To begin to generate high-quality questions, students must move beyond simply noticing what happens in a text to how authors achieve certain effects and why. In many close reading situations, generating questions can be a whole-class activity. However, teachers should also prepare students to accomplish this step independently. Once the class generates an analytical reading question, students read the text again to discover specific evidence that will help them answer that question. As they move into the next stages of close reading—discussing and processing—students will have substantial evidence to engage in that process.

Chapter 4: Comprehension Questions

1. Why is generating questions an important step in the close reading process?

2. What three steps can help students generate analytical reading questions?

3. Why is gradually increasing the challenge of close reading passages important for emerging analytical readers?

4. In what ways is step 4, reading analytically (in response to questions from step 3), different from step 2, reading twice and annotating?

Chapter 5

DISCUSSING AS A CLASS OR ANALYZING INDIVIDUALLY, AND USING PROCESSING ACTIVITIES

Once students develop evidence from reading the text analytically, the next step is to draw conclusions. Students will work with this evidence to provide answers to the questions from previous steps and begin to assemble meaning. If *analysis* means breaking something down into its constituent parts and examining those parts to learn something new, these next steps might be likened to *synthesis*—considering the evidence holistically to create a hypothesis about meaning and significance. But the discussing and processing step often gets missed, either due to time constraints or because we allow students to focus too often on "what" questions rather than "why" and "how" questions that demand discussion and processing. This step may be done as a class or by individual students; having students work independently is certainly important since this is how they must operate in a testing situation. Students who have well-developed discussion skills as part of the close reading process will develop the ability to analyze their own ideas in a testing situation. The same suggestions made about earlier stages in this process apply here: teachers should start students with lots of class discussion and modeling but give them plenty of opportunities to work alone as well.

In this chapter, we begin by examining how students process their uncovered evidence, focusing closely on the way the teacher can lead this process through proper questioning, with the ultimate goal of developing students' skills so they will have the independence to do this step on their own. Then, we look at ways to encourage students to create strong, defensible hypotheses about meaning and significance. Finally, we explore activities that prompt students to process their hypotheses to ensure their ideas are strong and accurate.

Discussing as a Class or Analyzing Individually

At this point, students have completed the analysis stage and created hypotheses regarding the close reading passage. It is now time for discussion of their work. In general, this is a whole-class activity, with students reacting to and questioning each other's ideas. In this way, a healthy analytical atmosphere should permeate the classroom and encourage all students to participate. It is important to achieve this often in the classroom because in a testing situation, students need confidence in using their own judgment to evaluate their own ideas.

In the early stages of promoting class discussion, the suggestion offered previously applies; there is safety in numbers, so have students work together (in small groups or pairs) to refine hypotheses and evaluate each other's work. This will encourage more participation. Teachers should monitor the groups' work, which often will provide teachers with a good idea of which students have developed good answers and which have taken a wrong turn. Initially, it will help if teachers choose fruitful ideas for class discussion. Eventually, however, the class must examine incorrect ideas and offer suggestions for improvement.

After asking one student (or one group) to offer a hypothesis, the teacher should encourage him or her to support the claim with specific textual evidence. In a way, this is like presenting a case in a courtroom. There is a claim, and there is backing in the form of specific textual evidence. This gives students the opportunity to truly work on their self-efficacy regarding their analytical skills. The degree to which their evidence supports their claim will encourage their self-confidence.

In general, the rest of the class should allow the students presenting their hypotheses and evidence to fully present this information before any discussion or challenge. This is simply good manners, and it may be that the students offering their ideas anticipate the objections and will offer answers before the discussion. During the discussion, the other students in the class play a key role. Their task is to listen carefully and analyze the quality of the argument and evidence. They should ask questions and even raise objections if they feel something has been missed or misinterpreted.

Through this discussion, students will gain understanding of the analysis process, the way evidence works to support ideas, the way to judge the quality of the evidence, and, most important, their own accuracy in analyzing the text. These discussions should happen often, and the teacher should carefully guide them so the atmosphere is supportive and intellectually safe. Two sets of guidelines are helpful: (1) guidelines for class discussions and (2) guidelines for teacher questions.

Guidelines for Class Discussions

Class discussions are opportunities for collaboration among members of a community. In the case of a close reading discussion, the class will be discussing a deeply considered community-read text. For discussions to be productive, there must be some ground rules or protocols. Further, the objective of a class discussion is to hear from the community, and that requires a wide range of voices in the room. A class discussion should never devolve into a conversation among three or four people.

As a part of training students for class discussion, it is important for the teacher to establish proper protocols for classroom behavior. One vital first step is to draw the distinction between *debate* and *discussion*. The teacher cannot allow the class atmosphere to devolve into "I'm right; you're wrong." Class discussion is not a contest; it's a collaborative examination of ideas. Teachers should directly teach students how to constructively respond to other students' ideas. These protocols should allow students to ask others to further explain their thinking, dig deeply into other students' ideas, and challenge others as long as they do so constructively without making personal attacks. Teachers can develop protocols based on the needs of their classes, but some recommended suggestions are as follows.

- Everyone in the discussion deserves respect.
- Everyone should participate in the discussion.
- No one should dominate the discussion.
- In responding to someone, start by positively identifying one or two ideas to build on.
- Rather than challenging someone's ideas, raise a question such as, "Have you considered . . . ?"

- Ask others to support their ideas with evidence. Ask, "Can you explain why you have taken the position you just stated?" or "Can you point to the evidence that supports your position?"

- Keep the discussion on topic. Try not to stray from the discussion with personal reactions or stories.

- Talk with each other, not just the person who is conducting the discussion.

- Speak clearly and calmly. Strong emotions can derail the discussion.

- In reacting to another student, try paraphrasing. For example, "Let me try to restate what you just said, and please correct me if I get it wrong . . ."

- Ask for help to understand others' ideas by stating, "Please help me understand what you are saying . . ."

It is essential to create guidelines such as these, make them known to students, and enforce them in order to generate productive discussions.

As mentioned previously, students must feel comfortable taking risks during the close reading process, especially during discussions. Teachers must foster a growth mindset in class discussions. A *growth mindset* refers to the belief that intelligence is changeable (Dweck, 2006). Individuals with a growth mindset believe that hard work can increase their intelligence and abilities. In other words, being wrong is not a tragedy; being wrong is an opportunity for growth. The worst situation that can happen is that making an error discourages further participation. Teachers should show students who present insupportable or incorrect answers the ways parts of their answers are right and thank them for offering their ideas. While not every idea bears fruit, every idea is important to the discussion. Teachers must make it comfortable for students in a class discussion to say what they think and be wrong. It is a step on the path to being correct.

If necessary, consider some specific instructional strategies to encourage positivity and a growth mindset in the classroom, such as those in the following list. *Motivating and Inspiring Students* (Marzano, Scott, Boogren, & Newcomb, 2017) offers details about such strategies.

- **Use intentionally inviting language:** Lead the class in a friendly manner. Speak to all students with respect, and give them input on the functioning of the classroom. Invite students to share personal interests.

- **Consider a class bill of rights:** Work with students to create a list of non-negotiable statements such as, "We all have the right to learn" and "We all have the right to be treated fairly."

- **Practice simple courtesies:** Do little things to show affection for students, such as smiling at them, greeting them when they arrive in class, inquiring how they are, and so on. Use appropriate physical contact, such as high fives, handshakes, or pats on the shoulder.

- **Stress academic equity:** Ensure all students have the opportunity to succeed. Challenge all students. Provide scaffolding for those who have more difficulty answering challenging questions.

- **Encourage a growth mindset:** Teach students directly about the growth mindset. Ask them to identify their own mindsets about different academic activities. Prompt them to adjust their thinking as needed.

Taken together, these guidelines create a safe and inviting environment for healthy, productive discourse.

Guidelines for Teacher Questions

Another key for teachers to guide a productive discussion is asking the right questions. Sometimes students can identify important literary elements in texts but stumble a bit to know what to do with that information. Consider the process of creating meaning from the data as a kind of experimentation. Once students observe something intriguing, they then posit a hypothesis and test their explanation. Placing the process of generating meaning in this context helps students see the steps of the process and allows them to see it as a manageable task, rather than an overwhelming one.

Teachers can help students develop the ability to process data effectively by asking the right kind of questions. Too often teachers ask students to identify the *what* of an author's work: What devices is she using in this passage? What words did the author choose? What is the theme or tone of this passage? Teachers should have students devote more time to answering the *how* and *why* of various effects: How does the author create the tone of this passage? Why would the author choose to use this tone in this passage? Those questions are central to, indeed the end points of, analytical techniques. Teachers can help students accomplish this with questioning that encourages students' own abilities but at the same time drives them deeper into the text.

Questioning at this level continually draws out student response. It is important that the teacher watch what is happening in the students' reasoning and try, to as great an extent as possible, to let students find the answers themselves. This isn't always possible, but it often is—with the right questions. The right questions take into account where the student is in his or her understanding of the passage, then take that understanding to the next increment—the next step in creating meaning and significance.

Teachers create their questions in many ways. Often teachers prepare the questions they will ask as part of their discussion lesson preparation. In general, teachers should avoid creating questioning sequences that lead students to the correct interpretation of the text. Part of the value of the close reading process stems from students creating their own questions and resulting analysis, and perfecting their own abilities to see when they are correct and when they have misinterpreted something. However, students who are just learning the analysis step do need some teacher guidance. Properly formed questions that suggest the correct direction (rather than the correct interpretation) can be helpful in the early stages of analysis but should be abandoned once students start to trust their own judgment a bit.

One reason teachers should resist the notion of the correct interpretation is that there likely is not only one. As stated previously, an interpretation is correct if it has solid textual evidence. Traditional interpretations are important, but they are not the only correct interpretations, and teachers must be open to this.

In general, and especially after initial instruction on analysis, teachers can rely on creating their questions on the fly as the discussion develops. Part of the challenge of leading a strong, productive class discussion on a close reading passage is to develop the ability to stay several cognitive steps ahead of the students. Teachers should not only be thinking about the implications of what a student is saying as he or she says it but also considering how the student arrived at the idea. The teacher might ask him- or herself questions such as the following.

- "What process did the student use to reach this conclusion?"

- "Are the assumptions behind the conclusion valid?"

- "If not, is this the moment to challenge the student?"

- "Can I guide the student to challenge his or her own assumptions by asking a slightly different question?"

The skill of creating these kinds of discussion responses takes much practice, and teachers won't always succeed. Just as teachers are patient with students, they must be patient with themselves.

As an example of the kind of responses a teacher might provide as guidance for students during a group discussion, consider again our ongoing example. Perhaps the discussion has narrowed to the opening sentence of the passage from the Declaration of Independence:

> We hold these truths to be self-evident, that all men are created equal, that they are endowed by their Creator with certain unalienable Rights, that among these are Life, Liberty and the pursuit of Happiness. (United States, 1776, para. 2)

A student is commenting on some of the diction in this sentence and says, "It seems to me that the author of this sentence is making a really powerful statement here, claiming that these rights come from God. That wouldn't be what the British would have thought, so in saying that, the author is suggesting for the first time a difference that will lead to a break with England."

There are some important insights in the student's statement, and the teacher would want to honor those. These insights include the boldness of the statement and the fact that it is different than the position the British might take. But the conclusion is impulsive. It is not clear from the passage that a difference in how one thinks about the endowment of individual rights would lead directly to a break with Britain. Indeed, if that were true, the rest of the passage, with its careful building of evidence, might be much less important.

As discussion leader, the teacher's task now is to formulate a question that redirects the student but avoids suggesting that he or she is incorrect or impulsive in his or her conclusion. That would be embarrassing and cause exactly the opposite student response the teacher wishes to elicit. The teacher must consider what response is desired for the student to re-examine whether the strength of his or her evidence (that the author claims individual rights come from God) is sufficiently strong for the conclusion (that it would lead to a claim that the colonies should break from Britain).

After responding in a positive way about the student's quality thinking (seeing the boldness of the statement and the fact that it is different than the position the British might take), the teacher might defuse the negativity of challenging the student's thinking by asking something out of context. For example, the teacher's next question to the entire class might be the following: "What does it take to change your mind about something? Let me clarify that: if you have taken a strong position on something, at what point do you feel like you can change your mind?"

This might seem like a diversion from the discussion at hand, but in the end, it is directly related to the question of re-examining evidence. People change their minds when evidence convinces them that they are likely wrong. When the class responds with that idea, the teacher would follow up with a question closer to the issue at hand: "What makes evidence that powerful? When does evidence become so powerful that it causes us to rethink a decision we have made?"

The class will likely respond by suggesting that there must be substantial, solid, and unchallenge-able evidence. At this point, the teacher can ask the entire class to use that criteria to re-examine the initial conclusion about this sentence. Note the teacher asks *all students* to engage in the process of re-examination, not just the one student. In returning the discussion to the sentence of the Declaration, the teacher can then ask the students to comment on the conclusion they themselves are drawing about the sentence and, in the process, re-examine the issue of whether this sentence is powerful enough to suggest a break with Britain.

Using Processing Activities

At some point following careful and deep processing (at the individual or class level), it is time to work with the students' conclusions. Teachers could ask students to simply decide the overall conclusions from any discussion, or they can use this discussion as a starting point for additional class activities, such as applying the analysis to a larger portion of the text (or the complete work) or for a writing activity.

Whatever form this task takes, a processing activity is critical. Students need to understand the point of close reading and see that careful analysis, in addition to the immediate work of close reading, has a larger impact—an application that eventually provides the incentive to keep analyzing the passage at hand. Eventually, students will begin to see that texts, even at the micro level of the close reading, will yield ideas with implications in other works of literature, nonfiction texts, fields of study, and life itself.

One common and often important processing activity is contextualizing the close reading passage within a general understanding of the larger text. Students should understand that close reading is dependent on the context of the passage.

Putting a Passage in Context

Even at lower secondary grades, students must develop this understanding, or they will begin to accept virtually any reading of a passage that seems grounded in the details as valid. Once students have analyzed the passage for detailed evidence and determined a meaning for the passage, it is important for them to engage in a final reading of the entire piece (whenever possible) and ask the key question, "Does our analysis of the close reading passage help us understand anything more about the entire text?"

To see how processing can proceed in the classroom, let's return to our example of the passage from the Declaration of Independence. Once again, here is the segment we used for our close reading activity:

> We hold these truths to be self-evident, that all men are created equal, that they are endowed by their Creator with certain unalienable Rights, that among these are Life, Liberty and the pursuit of Happiness.—That to secure these rights, Governments are instituted among Men, deriving their just powers from the consent of the governed, —That whenever any Form of Government becomes destructive of these ends, it is the Right of the People to alter or to abolish it, and to institute new Government, laying its foundation on such principles and organizing its powers in such form, as to them shall seem most likely to effect their Safety and Happiness. Prudence, indeed, will dictate that Governments long established should not be changed for light and transient causes; and accordingly all experience hath shewn, that mankind are more disposed to suffer, while evils are sufferable, than to right themselves by abolishing the forms to which they are accustomed. But when a long train of abuses and usurpations, pursuing invariably the same Object evinces a design to reduce them under absolute Despotism, it is their right, it is their duty, to throw off such Government, and to provide new Guards for their future security.—Such has been the patient sufferance of these Colonies; and such is now the necessity which constrains them to alter their former Systems of Government. The history of the present King of Great Britain is a history of repeated injuries and usurpations, all having in direct object the establishment of an absolute Tyranny over these States. (United States, 1776, para. 2)

At the end of the analytical reading and discussion, the class, having examined this passage as an example of an argument and identified the elements of argumentation at work in the passage, will likely see it as a strong argument in favor of severing the political and economic ties that connected the colonies with Great Britain. Further, students would likely conclude that a series of increasingly strong pieces of evidence supports that argument. They might also see the passage as appropriate for the audience at the time, even though it is challenging to modern readers. The next step is to process these conclusions.

One activity would be to place the passage and the analytical reading in the context of the entire document. This is not always possible because close reading passages are sometimes taken from lengthy works like plays, novels, long essays, and epic poems. In this case, the entire work is not too long. The teacher would provide the entire text of the Declaration of Independence and ask the class to consider their interpretation of the close reading passage in the context of the entire document. The teacher might ask students questions such as the following.

- "Is our analytical reading of the close reading passage consistent with the meaning, tone, and purpose of the entire document?"

- "Given the context of the entire document, do we need to adjust our analytical reading of the passage? If so, what are those adjustments, and what do we learn about our own analytical process when we make those adjustments?"

Having examined the entire Declaration, students will likely see that the close reading passage fits well into the larger argument in the document and that it sets up the argument that develops in the rest of the document. Further, students who have analyzed the close reading passage will be well equipped to identify additional rhetorical devices at work in the larger document. The teacher could now lead a much more substantial discussion of the effectiveness of the Declaration with the class or have each student write an essay (describing the rhetorical effectiveness of the Declaration, focusing on the elements of argumentation), do a presentation on the entire document as argument, or complete a larger project on the document, perhaps within the historical context of America in 1776. This type of knowledge application allows students to process their findings.

Using Knowledge Application Lessons

Asking students to process their findings from the close reading analysis requires them to operate at the very highest level of cognitive activity, the kind reflected in what educational researcher and author Robert J. Marzano (2017) refers to as *knowledge application lessons*. There are many instructional strategies for lessons of this type, and several apply to processing information from close reading analysis.

One such process is *experimental inquiry*. Once students have discussed how their findings relate to the close reading passage as a whole, they can make predictions based on their analysis and test those predictions with the entire work (or with a larger passage of the work). The following questions reflect the six steps in the experimental inquiry process (Marzano Research, 2016a).

1. What is my prediction?

2. How will I test my prediction?

3. What do I expect to see if my prediction is correct?

4. What actually happened?

5. Did my prediction come true?

6. How has my thinking changed?

To perform this process with their close reading analysis, students make a prediction that applies their conclusions about purpose, technique, theme, or tone to the larger passage. When successful, students will gain a growing self-confidence in their ability to be accurate close readers.

For example, consider again the opening sentences of *The Hobbit*. Students will have hypothesized that Tolkien (1974) is at the very early stages of developing characterization through a strong narrator, even as the book opens:

> In a hole in the ground there lived a hobbit. Not a nasty, dirty, wet hole, filled with the ends of worms and an oozy smell, nor yet a dry, bare, sandy hole with nothing in it to sit down on or to eat: it was a hobbit-hole, and that means comfort. (p. 15)

As students consider the entire novel, they must continually test their hypothesis and make adjustments as they read. Examining the steps of experimental inquiry specifically for this passage might look as follows.

1. **What is my prediction?** Tolkien develops characters by using a strong narrator.

2. **How will I test my prediction?** Periodically (chapter by chapter), we will test our prediction that Tolkien's characterization is based in strong reporting by a first-person narrator and that the characterization primarily continues through that narrative voice.

3. **What do I expect to see if my prediction is correct?** Characterization in the novel proceeds in the same manner as found in the opening paragraph, with narration developing the details.

4. **What actually happened?** Students will discover that much of the characterization in the novel occurs in this manner, but they will also note that other characterizations are very important, including statements made about characters by other characters, things characters say, and, most important, the choices and actions characters take.

5. **Did my prediction come true?** The answer to this question will lie in the answer to the fourth question.

6. **How has my thinking changed?** Students will need to adjust their hypothesis to account for the additional evidence from the body of the novel, stating that Tolkien uses a strong narrator for characterization but also uses a variety of other characterization techniques.

Another process is decision making. *Decision-making tasks* involve creating a list of alternatives, examining the relative strengths and weaknesses of each alternative, and finally selecting the best one. The following questions reflect the seven steps in the decision-making process (Marzano Research, 2016a).

1. What alternatives am I considering?

2. What criteria am I using to select among alternatives?

3. What do I predict will be the best alternative?

4. Which alternatives came out on top?

5. Do the results fit with my original prediction?

6. If not, how should my thinking change?

7. What are my conclusions?

In applying this strategy to processing a close reading analysis, students would decide among strong alternative readings of the close reading passage. These can be teacher- or student-generated alternatives. There may be conflicting interpretations of the passage within the class that would lend themselves to the decision-making process, or the teacher or students can research interpretations of the passage and compare them. In carrying out such a comparison, a decision-making matrix such as the one in figure 5.1 can be helpful.

Criteria	Alternatives							
0–Does not meet the criterion at all 1–Meets criterion slightly 2–Meets criterion 3–Strongly meets criterion								
Total								

Source: Marzano Research, 2016a, p. 13.

Figure 5.1: Decision-making matrix.

Let's look at an example of the use of a decision-making matrix with our passage from the Declaration of Independence. Suppose two alternative interpretations have emerged in class discussion of the following two sentences from our passage:

> Prudence, indeed, will dictate that Governments long established should not be changed for light and transient causes; and accordingly all experience hath shewn, that mankind are more disposed to suffer, while evils are sufferable, than to right themselves by abolishing the forms to which they are accustomed. But when a long train of abuses and usurpations, pursuing invariably the same Object evinces a design to reduce them under absolute Despotism, it is their right, it is their duty, to throw off such Government, and to provide new Guards for their future security.

One interpretation suggests that under the surface meaning of these sentences, there is a hint at the potential need to eliminate American slavery in the colonies—perhaps once they become their own nation. The other interpretation advocates a reading that supports only the surface meaning of the text, as an attack solely on the abuses of the British government on the American colonies. Those advocating the first reading point to "mankind are more disposed to suffer" and suggest that in the context of colonial life, *suffer* is so strong a word that it would evoke a resonance with the colonists that would indicate reference to slavery. Further, they have argued that in the second sentence, "it is their right, it is their duty, to throw off such Government," refers to slavery in the same manner.

While class discussion might resolve the issue, a decision-making matrix could assist students in determining the correct interpretation. Obviously, the criteria teachers use are vital in establishing which interpretation is most likely to be correct. In choosing these criteria, teachers should rely on rhetorical devices that are the basis of close reading. In this case, we might ask students to consider audience, purpose, occasion, and style (to include any rhetorical devices in the passage under consideration). The decision-making matrix might then look like figure 5.2.

Criteria	Alternatives	
0–Does not meet the criterion at all 1–Meets criterion slightly 2–Meets criterion 3–Strongly meets criterion	Passage references slavery	Passage does not reference slavery
Audience for the passage	0	2
Purpose of the passage	0	2
Occasion for the passage	0	2
Style (including literary devices)	1	0
Total	1	6

Figure 5.2: An example decision-making matrix containing criteria.

While class discussion would have to clarify each of the scores on this matrix, students should be able to see that the Declaration of Independence was written to the British government (specifically to King George III) for the purpose of declaring the American colonies as independent states. On an occasion in which formal style is meant to convey the seriousness of the argument for independence, the stylistic elements discovered by those advocating the inclusion of slavery as a secondary topic probably constitute a misreading of those elements, since they do not align with purpose, audience, or occasion.

As another example, consider the various readings of Shelley's (1818/1992) *Frankenstein*. The cited edition of this book contains essays on a number of alternative readings of the novel, including Marxist (described on pages 11–12), reader-response, feminist, and psychoanalytical approaches. After examining a close reading passage or two from the novel, a teacher might present students with these four alternative readings and ask them to decide which is most applicable for an important chapter, or perhaps for the entire novel. There may not be a single valid conclusion to this process since all of the readings may have value in themselves. However, students, in making the decision about validity, will find themselves deeply examining their own approaches to the interpretation of literature and will gain insights to their own lenses as they continue the close reading process.

Summary

In this chapter, we explored the final steps of the close reading process: discussing and processing. These steps are essential for students to cement their analyses and apply their understandings beyond the short passage. Teachers must foster a healthy environment for class discussion and lead the conversation by asking good questions that help students draw their own conclusions. Processing activities take many forms, but often involve examining the close reading passage and analysis in the context of the entire work. At the end of the close reading process, students will have a deeper understanding of the intricate nature of the texts they examine, and they will gain confidence in their own abilities to analyze increasingly challenging texts.

Chapter 5: Comprehension Questions

1. How is creating meaning from a close reading passage related to the process of generating and testing a hypothesis?

2. Should teachers plan the questions they will use in an analytical discussion? Why, or why not?

3. What are the steps in helping students draw strong conclusions from an analysis of a close reading text?

4. What is the teacher's role when students are discussing their hypotheses regarding their close reading analysis?

5. Why is processing an important step of the close reading process, and what are some effective ways the teacher can ask students to process their understanding of a passage?

Chapter 6

PLANNING AND ASSESSING CLOSE READING

As teachers bring the close reading process into the classroom, they must consider the lesson sequence that will introduce students to the process and then build their abilities. As stated at the start of this book, close reading is not a process that teachers can introduce to students and perfect in a single unit or even a single school year; teachers must continually reinforce the close reading process from year to year. Each year, teachers will want to ensure students are completely familiar with the process and work on building their close reading proficiency.

In this chapter, we will look at how teachers use a proficiency scale to determine student performance scores in close reading and how to share that information with students. Finally, we will take a brief look at how teachers integrate close reading into unit planning and how they might assess close reading.

Measuring Student Progress in Close Reading

As with any skill they need to practice and develop, students will be at different levels at different times. A useful way to help students understand the level they should reach to become proficient in close reading (as well as their status on the journey to that proficiency) is through a proficiency scale (Marzano, 2010; Marzano, 2017; Marzano, Norford, Finn, & Finn, 2017). A *proficiency scale* defines different levels of ability relative to a skill or a body of content. It presents a description of a learning progression regarding particular content, in this case, the skill of close reading. Figure 6.1 shows the generic form of a proficiency scale.

4.0	Advanced content
3.0	Target content
2.0	Simpler content necessary for proficiency
1.0	With help, partial success with score 2.0 content and score 3.0 content
0.0	Even with help, no success

Figure 6.1: Generic form of a proficiency scale.

Score 3.0 content is the focus of the proficiency scale because it is the *target content*—the level of knowledge and skill students are expected to master. Score 2.0 is the basic information and procedures teachers directly teach students as they are beginning to work with the content. Score 4.0 represents advanced applications that go beyond what teachers expect or teach in class.

In the case of close reading, one can define score 3.0 proficiency as the ability of the student to fully use all six steps of the close reading process as an integrated member of the class. This means the student will work independently at times and with others at other times to read, analyze, and develop accurate interpretations of a close reading passage. At score 2.0, students will be learning the basic content of the close reading process. This includes learning specific vocabulary for the close reading process, learning each of the six steps, and practicing applying those six steps in isolation, perhaps in teacher-directed activities. A student who scores 4.0 (beyond proficiency) can do every step independently. Figure 6.2 shows a possible proficiency scale for developing the skill of close reading analysis.

4.0	The student can independently and accurately use all six steps of the close reading process and apply them to texts beyond grade level in a variety of academic situations.
3.0	The student can accurately use all six steps of the close reading process, arriving at a correct and well-supported analytical interpretation of a grade-level-appropriate close reading passage.
2.0	The student can recognize and recall specific vocabulary important to close reading analysis. Informational text: *logos appeal, ethos appeal, pathos appeal, claim, grounds, backing, qualifiers* Literary text: *plot, character, point of view, setting, tone, figurative language, theme, central meaning* The student can perform basic processes such as: Apply each of the six steps in the close reading process in teacher-directed activities.
1.0	With help, the student has partial success at score 2.0 content and score 3.0 content.
0.0	Even with help, the student has no success.

Figure 6.2: Proficiency scale for close reading.

This scale is simply an example, and teachers may wish to modify it or use a different one to reflect the specific content focus at each level. For example, teachers could add or substitute different vocabulary terms at score 2.0.

One advantage of using a proficiency scale as students learn a new skill is their increased understanding of what they need to know and be able to do, as well as their understanding of where they are in that learning progression. Of course, such understanding is only built through the continual use and reference to the proficiency scale during instruction, assessment, and feedback. Teachers should introduce the proficiency scale and its associated learning goal to students at the start of instruction on close reading. In the introductory lesson, the scale will provide the framework, so students will understand the process and their level of skill. As the unit proceeds and the teacher continues to instruct, assess, and provide feedback, he or she uses the proficiency scale as a reference point with students for each step. For example, the teacher might begin lessons by reviewing the proficiency scale and explaining which level of content the class is working with that day. Assessments might overtly reference the levels of the scale. As the teacher returns and reviews students' work, he or she provides feedback on their progress using the proficiency scale levels.

Students need to understand that the teacher measures student progress along the scale incrementally—that they will begin low and finish high, as does anyone who is learning a new skill. Teachers must continually reassure students that it's fine to start at 1.0 or 2.0 as long as they are working on getting to 3.0. Teachers should be sure to provide initial feedback concerning where students are starting on the four-point proficiency scale. Then, as further assessments and opportunities to practice close reading arise, students receive more feedback about their progress, and they can see the slow approach toward achievement of the learning goal. This is important in all standards-based learning, but particularly with a skill like close reading, which requires patience, as initial progress may be slow.

One highly effective technique for encouraging growth in the skill of close reading is student goal setting. Marzano (2010) noted that having students set and track progress on personal learning goals has been connected to a 32-percentile gain in student achievement on that goal. There are many methods for goal setting and tracking progress. Using a goal-setting and tracking form such as the one in figure 6.3 will encourage students to follow their own progress.

Name: _____

Freshman Literature and Composition
Goal-Tracking Sheet

Priority Standard: Close reading—The student can independently and accurately use all six steps of the close reading process, arriving at a correct and well-supported analytical interpretation of a grade-level-appropriate close reading passage.

Current score (out of 4): ____1.5____   Goal: ____3.0____ By _____end of semester one_____ (date)

In order to accomplish the above goal, I will do the following:

__Form a study group with other students_____

__Come in for extra help_____

__Do extra practice in close reading_____

Goal tracking:

	A	B	C	D	E	F	G	H	I	J	K	L	M	N	O	P	Q	R	S	T	U	V	W	X	Y	Z
4.0																										
3.0																										
2.0	●																									
1.0																										
0.0																										

A: <u>Benchmark assessment August 22</u>   J: _____   S: _____

B: _____   K: _____   T: _____

C: _____   L: _____   U: _____

D: _____   M: _____   V: _____

E: _____   N: _____   W: _____

F: _____   O: _____   X: _____

G: _____   P: _____   Y: _____

H: _____   Q: _____   Z: _____

I: _____   R: _____

Figure 6.3: Student goal-tracking sheet.

Teachers using a goal-tracking sheet such as the one in figure 6.3 would start by assessing the students' initial proficiency in close reading using a proficiency scale such as the example in figure 6.2 (page 88; for more on assessment, see page 92). Teachers report scores using the proficiency scale. Once the teacher establishes a benchmark score for each student, he or she will distribute a goal-setting and tracking form to introduce students to the idea of setting personal goals. Students then set a goal for the close reading standard—one that is reasonable, given the instructional time available. Students need to have a thorough understanding of the proficiency scale in order to do this. The teacher might also choose to print the close reading proficiency scale on the same sheet as the goal-tracking form so students can always reference it. In setting their goals, students may enlist the advice of the teacher, but it is important that students make the final decisions about their own goals since they will be holding themselves to that standard. A vital discussion regarding the actions students will take to support their goals follows. Students should identify specific actions they can take—beyond simply coming to class ready to learn—such as working together in study groups outside of class, assigning themselves additional practice, and seeking out the teacher for additional help. Again, teachers should encourage the class to identify these goals for themselves, as they will have to take the action to accomplish the tasks.

Next, students record their benchmark assessment score and the date on line A of the sheet (see figure 6.3, page 89). This will be the starting point for recording their progress. Throughout the unit, semester, or year, the teacher provides frequent opportunities for students to assess their progress and record their scores on the goal-tracking sheet. Every assessment on this sheet must align with the close reading proficiency scale.

At first, students may be reticent about using such a tracking sheet. Share the research with them and assure them that following this procedure will increase their close reading abilities. Once students consistently use this form, some important changes often occur. The language students use regarding their involvement with their own learning changes. They speak less in terms of the grade and more in terms of their own learning progression. Even more important, a goal-tracking form such as the one in figure 6.3 helps enormously in encouraging the development of student self-efficacy regarding a challenging skill such as close reading. Students will understand their own progress in developing their close reading abilities, and a setback will seem much less devastating when they are aware of their overall progress.

Planning for Close Reading

To teach a skill such as close reading, some fundamental shifts occur when teachers plan from a learning target rather than from specific course content. In standards-based learning, individual lesson planning is less important than the sequence of activities and assessments in a unit plan. Close reading is a skill that students will likely develop across multiple units of course content. Thus, in planning to develop the skill of close reading in students, teachers should take a broader view, seeing development across a longer period.

Marzano (2017), in *The New Art and Science of Teaching*, identified three different kinds of lessons teachers use during a typical unit. *Direct instruction lessons* are those in which teachers identify critical content, and chunk that content into small pieces students can process. Teachers directly teach instructional lessons through lecture, demonstration, or the use of some media that introduces new content to students. Once students process this new information, teachers typically move into *practicing and deepening lessons,* in which students engage in different kinds of activities to develop their abilities to engage with the content at a deeper and more rigorous level. Finally, teachers will move on to *knowledge application lessons,* where students work more independently to develop their abilities to apply their new knowledge or skill in novel ways. Teachers often use knowledge application activities with small groups. Each of these three lesson types has associated instructional strategies. Marzano (2017) identified many useful teaching strategies for all three types of lessons, including previewing, highlighting critical information, reviewing content, reflecting on learning, and assigning purposeful homework.

Teachers can use the close reading proficiency scale (see figure 6.2, page 88) to help plan instruction. Typically, teachers will use direct instruction lessons for score 2.0 content and, to some extent, score 3.0 content. For example, as teachers share the steps of the close reading process with students and ensure they understand and can execute each step at a basic level, teachers would likely employ direct instruction to introduce and reinforce score 2.0 content. Once students have this basic ability, the teacher will gradually move them to practicing and deepening lessons, where they will work on the 3.0 level descriptor, "The student can accurately use all six steps of the close reading process, arriving at a correct and well-supported analytical interpretation of a grade-level-appropriate close reading passage." Finally, teachers will use knowledge application lessons for further practice with score 3.0 content or to give students the chance to achieve performance at level 4.0.

Although teachers will likely introduce the entire close reading process to students at the start of a unit so they have familiarity with the overall sequence of steps, each step also needs specific instruction. For example, a teacher might design a sequence of lessons on step 1 of the close reading process, prereading. Figure 6.4 depicts an example of a prereading lesson sequence. This approach allows students to understand and practice the new skill, in this case (see figure 6.4) step 1 of the close reading process, before the teacher introduces them to the details of the next step.

Lesson One	Introduce the concept of prereading and offer one or two typical strategies. (DI)
	Students practice one of the prereading strategies as a whole class and debrief their response. (DI)
Lesson Two	Review the concept of prereading and the steps of the practiced prereading strategy. (All)
	Teachers provide guided practice with the strategy. (All)
	Students practice the strategy independently on a new text, comparing their reactions with peers and evaluating the accuracy of their process. (PD)
	Teachers apply the strategy to a homework text and note student successes and challenges.
Lesson Three	Teachers debrief student successes and challenges on the homework text. Teachers review any aspects of the strategy that need clarification. (All)
	Assessment of step 1: prereading. Students independently apply the prereading strategy and self-correct as the teacher reviews the assessment in class. Students self-assess their progress on step 1. (Assess)
	Teacher introduces step 2 of the close reading process—reading twice and annotating. (DI)

Key:
DI—Direct instruction, PD—Practicing and deepening, All—Instructional strategies that apply to all lessons, Assess—Assessment

Figure 6.4: Example of a lesson sequence on prereading.

When designing lesson sequences, teachers will want to keep in mind the overall learning progression in the proficiency scale. If students start from almost no ability in close reading, the teacher will want to spend considerably more time instructing at the 2.0 level. If students have some previously developed ability in close reading, the teacher might quickly revisit score 2.0 content, and then move to score 3.0 and possibly 4.0. The teacher's understanding of the abilities of each student in the class will help him or her make these decisions.

It is important to note that close reading abilities will sometimes greatly vary across the class. In one class there may be students who are just getting started with close reading, while others are on the verge of independently applying close reading to texts beyond grade level. Because of the nature of the learning progression, close reading provides teachers the opportunity to differentiate activities for the individual abilities of the class members. Thus, while some students work independently on close reading activities, the teacher can work directly with students still learning the basics.

Assessing Close Reading

Close reading, by its very nature, requires a comprehensive form of assessment. Like the assessment of writing, the close reading process does not provide the student with a series of separate assessment items at each proficiency scale level. Yet, it is possible to assess students at various stages of their learning progression on that proficiency scale, and there are opportunities to use different forms of assessment at different stages of the student's learning. In using a proficiency scale to judge a student's status in the learning progression for close reading, the aim is to identify the level (that is, 0.0, 1.0, 2.0, 3.0, or 4.0) of that student. The judgment of that assessment should align with the levels of the proficiency scale.

There are two ways to go about this: leveled assessments and holistic assessments. *Leveled assessments* include items and tasks that measure student performance at a single level of the scale. For example, one assessment might focus on score 2.0, with items that determine whether the student is proficient in each portion of the content at level 2.0 on the scale. Because score 2.0 content focuses on vocabulary and basic processes, level 2.0 items might ask students to provide definitions of key terms or require students to apply steps of the close reading process in a teacher-directed manner. A student who completes these items successfully would be at level 2.0 on the proficiency scale. Figure 6.5 gives an example of level 2.0 items.

Match each definition with the letter of the correct term.

1. Exceptions to arguments that indicate the degree of certainty of the argument   _____   a. Logos appeal

2. An argument that focuses on emotion   _____   b. Ethos appeal

3. A new idea or opinion   _____   c. Pathos appeal

4. An argument that focuses on reason   _____   d. Claim

5. Information or facts that help establish the validity of the grounds   _____   e. Grounds

6. The initial evidence for an argument   _____   f. Backing

7. An argument that focuses on morality   _____   g. Qualifier

For the following questions, please refer to this close reading passage:

> *When in the Course of human events it becomes necessary for one people to dissolve the political bonds which have connected them with another, and to assume among the powers of the earth, the separate and equal station to which the Laws of Nature and of Nature's God entitle them, a decent respect to the opinions of mankind requires that they should declare the causes which impel them to the separation. (U.S. Declaration of Independence, 1776, para. 1)*

Here are definitions of some words used in the passage you might not know:

Course—history
station—place
dissolve—break
entitle—deserving
bonds—connections
impel—move

8. **Prereading:** What do you already know about this passage? Please record your reactions and thoughts here.

9. **Reading twice and annotating:** Read the passage twice, and mark areas of question or interest.

   When in the Course of human events it becomes necessary for one people to dissolve the political bands which have connected them with another, and to assume among the powers of the earth, the separate and equal station to which the Laws of Nature and of Nature's God entitle them, a decent respect to the opinions of mankind requires that they should declare the causes which impel them to the separation.

10. **Generating questions:** Considering your annotations from the previous step, please make an initial attempt to answer this focus question—What is the purpose of this passage?

    Please provide a reason or two for your answer.

11. **Reading analytically:** Read the passage with the focus question in mind. Annotate (with comments) anything important.

    Focus question: What is the purpose of this passage?

    When in the Course of human events it becomes necessary for one people to dissolve the political bands which have connected them with another, and to assume among the powers of the earth, the separate and equal station to which the Laws of Nature and of Nature's God entitle them, a decent respect to the opinions of mankind requires that they should declare the causes which impel them to the separation.

    Looking through your annotations, what is your answer now to the focus question? Please provide evidence from your work.

12. **Discussing and processing:** Answer each of the following questions using the information you found in your close reading of the passage.

    a. The purpose of this passage is most likely:

       To state the author's conclusion

       To generate sympathy for the author's cause

       To introduce the reason for the document that follows

       To provide reasons for the author's argument

    b. The tone of this passage can best be described as:

       Formal

       Personal

       Realistic

       Angry

Figure 6.5: Sample assessment for score 2.0 content.

The assessment in figure 6.5 measures students' ability to recall and use the vocabulary and basic steps of the close reading process. It is likely the teacher would use this assessment early in the learning cycle, perhaps after instruction on all steps of the process but before students have had many opportunities to practice the process. It is not necessary to assess all of the score 2.0 content on every score 2.0 assessment. A teacher might give one assessment on the vocabulary portion and another on the six steps of the process. Recall, however, that the purpose of the assessments is for the teacher to gain enough information about student performance to make an educated inference about where the student is on the proficiency scale. In order to assign a score of 2.0, for example, the student must have mastered all of the level 2.0 content; thus, at some point the teacher must assess all the content.

Later, when students are more adept at the process, the teacher might assess level 3.0 performance. Students working at level 3.0 on the close reading proficiency scale would be able to independently apply all six levels of the close reading process to a grade-level passage. An assessment of score 3.0 content might present a single grade-level short close reading passage and ask the student to perform each of the six steps, recording in writing his or her work so the teacher can make a judgment about the performance of each step. If the student accurately completes each step of the process on a grade-level passage, it is safe to say the student is performing at level 3.0. Figure 6.6 provides an example of such an assessment.

Use the six steps of the close reading process to read and analyze the following passage. Be sure to show your work in each step. The steps are listed, and the passage is copied for your annotation at each step.

Close reading passage:

We, therefore, the Representatives of the united States of America, in General Congress, Assembled, appealing to the Supreme Judge of the world for the rectitude of our intentions, do, in the Name, and by Authority of the good People of these Colonies, solemnly publish and declare, That these united Colonies are, and of Right ought to be Free and Independent States; that they are Absolved from all Allegiance to the British Crown, and that all political connection between them and the State of Great Britain, is and ought to be totally dissolved; and that as Free and Independent States, they have full Power to levy War, conclude Peace, contract Alliances, establish Commerce, and to do all other Acts and Things which Independent States may of right do. — And for the support of this Declaration, with a firm reliance on the protection of divine Providence, we mutually pledge to each other our Lives, our Fortunes, and our sacred Honor. (U.S. Declaration of Independence, 1776, para. 32)

Here are definitions of some words used in the passage you might not know.

Assembled—meeting together
solemnly—seriously
rectitude—correctness
Absolved—free from

Step 1: Prereading

Step 2: Reading twice and annotating

We, therefore, the Representatives of the united States of America, in General Congress, Assembled, appealing to the Supreme Judge of the world for the rectitude of our intentions, do, in the Name, and by Authority of the good People of these Colonies, solemnly publish and declare, That these united Colonies are, and of Right ought to be Free and Independent States; that they are Absolved from all Allegiance to the British Crown, and that all political connection between them and the State of Great Britain, is and ought to be totally dissolved; and that as Free and Independent States, they have full Power to levy War, conclude Peace, contract Alliances, establish Commerce, and to do all other Acts and Things which Independent States may of right do. — And for the support of this Declaration, with a firm reliance on the protection of divine Providence, we mutually pledge to each other our Lives, our Fortunes, and our sacred Honor.

Step 3: Generating questions

Step 4: Reading analytically

We, therefore, the Representatives of the united States of America, in General Congress, Assembled, appealing to the Supreme Judge of the world for the rectitude of our intentions, do, in the Name, and by Authority of the good People of these Colonies, solemnly publish and declare, That these united Colonies are, and of Right ought to be Free and Independent States; that they are Absolved from all Allegiance to the British Crown, and that all political connection between them and the State of Great Britain, is and ought to be totally dissolved; and that as Free and Independent States, they have full Power to levy War, conclude Peace, contract Alliances, establish Commerce, and to do all other Acts and Things which Independent States may of right do. — And for the support of this Declaration, with a firm reliance on the protection of divine Providence, we mutually pledge to each other our Lives, our Fortunes, and our sacred Honor.

Step 5: Discussing as a class or analyzing individually

Step 6: Using processing activities

Figure 6.6: Sample assessment for score 3.0 content.

Finally, teachers can provide students with the opportunity to perform at level 4.0 by asking them to apply the six-step close reading process to a passage beyond grade level or outside the regular class content. For example, a ninth-grade English language arts student could apply the close reading process to a short passage from a more advanced text or from a social studies or science curriculum. If the student can independently and accurately apply the close reading process, that would constitute evidence of score 4.0 ability.

One advantage of using a leveled assessment is the focused clarity it provides about the student's performance on the learning progression. With separate assessments for each level of the scale, the student will reveal at which levels he or she can perform on the scale and which levels are not yet mastered. Teachers can also customize the assessment to the individual level of the student. This provides clear feedback to both the teacher and the student about the student's progress and can be useful information both for the teacher planning additional instruction and for the student understanding the progress made on personal learning goals. It would constitute valid feedback, which students can record on their goal-setting and tracking form (see figure 6.3, page 89, for an example).

Leveled assessments are helpful for both the teacher and student, but once students have moved past the early stages of learning to close read, another assessment format becomes a valid option. To introduce this option, consider an analogy to the assessment of writing ability. Once students have learned and practiced the skill of writing an essay, teachers expect them to write essays with little guidance. Students might be assigned a topic or given a rubric so they know what the teacher will look for, but they write on their own without structured steps. The teacher can assess the skill of close reading in a similarly independent manner.

This kind of assessment of close reading is called a *holistic assessment*—one in which the teacher assesses many aspects of the students' abilities in the close reading process at once. In this case, the teacher simply presents the passage to students and asks them to close read it. The passage can be a grade-level text to assess score 3.0 and below, or it can be more challenging to see if students have reached score 4.0. Teachers simply expect students to apply the close reading process without indicating the steps and then report their findings. Usually this takes the form of a written response that requires students to use evidence to support their conclusions. Alternatively, teachers could ask students to present their findings orally or engage in a debate.

In scoring a holistic assessment, teachers use the close reading proficiency scale as a rubric and make a judgment regarding the scale level of the student's performance. Although it may appear much more subjective, in fact, the proficiency scale provides clear divisions between student performances at each level and ensures a common understanding of both teacher and student of the student's performance at each level. Thus, feedback in the form of a four-point scale on a holistic assessment is valid, and students can record this information on their goal-setting and tracking forms.

In assessing a student's emerging abilities, the ideal assessment system might be a series of both leveled and holistic assessments. As teachers begin to teach the close reading process and the vocabulary at level 2.0, an assessment of content at that level is a good idea. Then, as students continue to apply and develop their abilities, the teacher could assess level 3.0 performance. Finally, a teacher could use a holistic assessment, perhaps of two passages—one at grade level and one beyond—where students close read the one they feel comfortable with to assess their abilities well into a close reading unit. If the student succeeds at the grade-level passage, he or she would be at level 3.0; a student who succeeds on the beyond-grade-level text would be at level 4.0. No matter the type of assessment, it is essential for teachers to provide students with numerous opportunities to demonstrate their close reading abilities.

Summary

In this chapter, we considered instruction and assessment as they relate to close reading. The foundation of instruction and assessment is the proficiency scale, which details several levels of knowledge and skill. Teachers can use the proficiency scale to plan instruction and as a way to compare student performance on a learning progression. As with any academic content or skill, students must receive direct instruction on close reading. Once the teacher has taught each step of the process, students can progress to practicing and deepening activities, and eventually to knowledge application. It is also important that teachers assess students' progress in close reading. Students should have multiple opportunities to demonstrate what they can do on both leveled and holistic assessments. Finally, students should set goals for themselves and track progress toward those goals.

Chapter 6: Comprehension Questions

1. What are the three types of lessons teachers typically use in a unit of instruction? How do teachers align lessons with the close reading proficiency scale?

2. What is the difference between a *leveled* assessment and a *holistic* assessment? How can teachers use these types of assessments?

3. How can teachers use personal goal setting and performance tracking to encourage student self-efficacy in learning a skill like close reading?

EPILOGUE

An ever-increasing demand for critical thinking in schools and the workplace challenges students today, who need tools to conduct that critical thinking. Close reading represents one of the most powerful tools teachers can develop in students to prepare them for this challenge. Further, the benefits of becoming an effective reader extend far beyond academic achievement. Students who have mastered close reading become strong thinkers, and they often enjoy applying those skills beyond the classroom. By showing students how much there is to gain from analyzing written texts, teachers are helping to develop lifelong readers and, therefore, lifelong learners. As educators, there is little we do in the classroom that is more important than this.

APPENDIX A

ANSWERS TO COMPREHENSION QUESTIONS

Answers to Chapter 2: Comprehension Questions

1. *What are some important considerations when choosing a passage for close reading?*

   Teachers should consider four important factors when choosing a close reading passage. First, they should consider the interests of both the students and the teacher. If teachers can connect with student interests, they are more likely to connect students with the passage. Also, if possible, teachers should choose a passage they can demonstrate enthusiasm about. Second, teachers should consider the complexity of the passage. Typically, the passage should meet the reading grade level of students, yet teachers should occasionally present students with a passage that challenges student abilities just a bit. Third, teachers must consider that informational and literary texts share many of the same devices and themes so they must teach all types of texts to students. Teachers should teach these texts together, rather than in genre-based units. Finally, the length of the passage is important. Teachers want a short but rich passage, which should usually fit on one side of an 8.5 × 11–inch piece of paper.

2. *What important steps should a teacher take in preparing to teach a close reading passage?*

   It is important for teachers to understand that the reading of the passage they prepare will not be the sole correct answer. Further, teachers should self-assess their own close reading abilities. The teacher should consider how to introduce the close reading process to students, including dealing with why it is necessary and modeling the six steps. If the student is a novice close reader, a checklist of devices may help.

3. *What is the difference between teacher-led and independent prereading strategies?*

   Teacher-led prereading strategies are ideal for students in the early stages of learning the close reading process. These strategies tend to be more teacher-dependent and focus on specific content in the close reading passage. Independent prereading strategies are more appropriate for experienced close readers and focus more on independence in preparing to close read.

4. *Describe four considerations for selecting the most appropriate prereading activity.*

   Teachers should consider the skill the close reading passage addresses and whether the prereading activity should be specific to that skill. Further, when the subject is the focus of the lesson, the teacher would design the prereading activity to access student background knowledge and opinions on that subject. A close reading passage might present a significant challenge to student abilities, and in this case, the teacher might select a teacher-led activity even for advanced students. Finally, a new genre may present students with a challenge they are not used to, and the teacher can choose a prereading activity to assist them with that challenge.

Answers to Chapter 3:
Comprehension Questions

1. *What are the differences in student actions between the first and second readings of the reading twice and annotating step of the close reading process?*

   In the first reading, students should focus on understanding the text and making initial annotations based on the subject and their background knowledge of the text. From this first reading, students should process their understanding and generate specific things to look for in the second reading. During the second reading, the student is focused on looking for those specific things, although they should remain open to new insights that may not have emerged in the first reading.

2. *What are some strategies to help students who find very little to annotate in their first and second readings of a close reading passage?*

   If students struggle to find evidence in the readings, teachers may suggest a number of strategies. A quick conversation with peers or a whole-class discussion may help. Encouraging students to look for simpler things rather than deep ideas may allow them to focus on more obvious aspects of the text. Trying a third or fourth reading or modeling a reading with students to identify elements to focus on will allow for a productive next reading. Finally, teachers should assure students that there is something to find. The passage does have value or the teacher wouldn't have chosen it, so the task is to dig it out.

3. *What criteria should students use to decide what to annotate as they read?*

   Teachers can provide many criteria to guide students learning to annotate, and these criteria will depend on the purpose of the close reading activity. Some of the criteria a teacher might provide can include a short passage, sentence, or phrase that seems significant in the context of the class's focus in reading the text, a piece of text that resonates with something the author emphasizes, a passage that generates a question for the reader, a rhetorical device that appears significant, or a quotation that is rich and relevant.

4. *How should students use their knowledge and experience with rhetorical devices in the reading twice and annotating step of the close reading process?*

   Assuming the teacher has taught students the various types of rhetorical devices, students can focus on identifying those devices in a close reading passage and understanding how the author is using the device. During the reading twice and annotating step, it is likely students will formulate a question about the use of a rhetorical device that will inform the next steps in the process. Fully analyzing the impact of a rhetorical device will require completion of the entire close reading process.

Answers to Chapter 4: Comprehension Questions

1. *Why is generating questions an important step in the close reading process?*

   Guiding students to ask analytical questions helps ensure their analytical reading focuses on areas of the text that will yield answers. Less dependent on personal reaction, analytical reading questions specifically help students encounter the passage at a micro level.

2. *What three steps can help students generate analytical reading questions?*

   After the reading twice and annotating step, teachers should (1) put students into groups to share their thoughts. Then, as a class or in groups, teachers should ask students to (2) combine and edit questions. Finally, after identifying one or more analytical reading questions, the teacher should (3) prepare students to read analytically for a specific question.

3. *Why is gradually increasing the challenge of close reading passages important for emerging analytical readers?*

   While students who are learning the close reading process need texts that provide success in their early efforts, it is vital for teachers to also challenge students' abilities. College- and adult-level reading centers on texts that constantly challenge readers, and students need strong abilities to read beyond the plot to the level of the author's argument, purpose, and method, even in literary texts.

4. *In what ways is step 4, reading analytically (in response to questions from step 3), different from step 2, reading twice and annotating?*

   Unlike the earlier reading twice and annotating stage, students close reading in the reading analytically stage are looking at the text for specific answers to their questions. This requires students to focus less on their personal reactions to the text and more on the *what* and *how* of the authorial choices. The result will be an examination of the text at the micro level and the collection of specific evidence from the text in support of an emerging answer to the reading analytically question.

Answers to Chapter 5: Comprehension Questions

1. *How is creating meaning from a close reading passage related to the process of generating and testing a hypothesis?*

   The creation of meaning from a close reading passage is analogous to generating and testing a hypothesis because both involve looking closely at something that intrigues the mind and, using the available data, formulating an explanation that requires further testing.

2. *Should teachers plan the questions they will use in an analytical discussion? Why, or why not?*

   In general, teachers should avoid planning their exact questions in advance. They should develop questions on the fly in response to the discussion as it develops. This is a challenging process, and teachers need to develop the skill of interpreting the student's reasoning and then responding with a question that gently leads the student to analyze his or her own thinking. In the case of beginning students, teachers can prepare some questions to help lead students toward a strong analytical discussion.

3. *What are the steps in helping students draw strong conclusions from an analysis of a close reading text?*

   The steps to helping students draw strong conclusions about the text are (1) examine the evidence, (2) look for patterns in the evidence, and (3) generate a hypothesis from the pattern in the evidence.

4. *What is the teacher's role when students are discussing their hypotheses regarding their close reading analysis?*

   While the teacher organizes and, to a certain extent, guides the discussion, students have the most important role in the discussion. Teachers should listen to the students' ideas and gauge the effectiveness of the support for their hypotheses, always being ready to redirect the conversation if it gets off track. Teachers should provide a supportive atmosphere by enacting protocols for a healthy discussion.

5. *Why is processing an important step of the close reading process, and what are some effective ways the teacher can ask students to process their understanding of a passage?*

   The processing step allows students to understand the point of the work and provides an important conclusion to the close reading process. Teachers can provide many effective processing activities, but they all should require students use the results of close reading to engage the text at a high cognitive level. Often, processing activities ask students to place their analytical reading of the passage in the context of the text as a whole. These activities may include, but aren't limited to, project presentations, deeper and broader analytical readings, essays, experimental inquiry, and decision making.

Answers to Chapter 6:
Comprehension Questions

1. *What are the three types of lessons teachers typically use in a unit of instruction? How do teachers align lessons with the close reading proficiency scale?*

   Teachers use direct instruction lessons to present new content, and these lessons usually apply to levels 2.0 and 3.0 on the proficiency scale. Practicing and deepening lessons involve different kinds of instructional strategies that allow students to develop their abilities at a more rigorous level and are usually at level 3.0 on the proficiency scale. Knowledge application lessons allow students to work independently to apply their knowledge in situations beyond the standard content of a course. Knowledge application lessons allow students to perform at level 4.0 on the proficiency scale.

2. *What is the difference between a* leveled *assessment and a* holistic *assessment? How can teachers use these types of assessments?*

   A *leveled* assessment presents separate assessment items for each level of the proficiency scale. A *holistic* assessment uses the entire scale to assess all items at once. In either case, the teacher uses the proficiency scale as a rubric, making a judgment about the student's performance on the levels of the scale. The teacher should use both types of assessment as students develop their close reading abilities.

3. *How can teachers use personal goal setting and performance tracking to encourage student self-efficacy in learning a skill like close reading?*

   Students setting goals and tracking their performance has been related to a 32 percentile gain in student achievement (Marzano, 2010). By having students set personal goals and use an associated tracking form to understand their progress in learning to apply the close reading process, students gain self-confidence in using this challenging skill.

Source: Marzano, R. J. (2010). Formative assessment & standards-based grading. *Bloomington, IN: Marzano Research.*

APPENDIX B

EXTENDED EXAMPLES OF CLOSE READING

While it is possible to describe the close reading process in general and come to an understanding of the steps and how to share them with students, sometimes the most effective means for deepening one's understanding is to observe the process used in the classroom. Acknowledging the limitations of a printed text, this appendix strives to provide such an experience. Here we observe a classroom and the teacher's interactions with students in the moment. This appendix provides three examples: two literary and one informational. In each case, there is both a discussion of the planning and execution of the process steps and a sample script of the class discussion with commentary exemplifying the teacher's processing of students' responses.

Literary Example 1

"Fog" by Carl Sandburg

Genre: Lyric poetry

Grade level: 7

Poetry is generally considered the most challenging kind of literary text. Unlike prose, poetry has its own rules and famously cannot be defined. The moment we say it is *this* or *that*, we can find an exception to the rule that rewrites the definition. Avoiding a definition of poetry, we can perhaps at least agree with the many critics who have stated that one advantage of poetry is that its language is strongly loaded with meaning, surface and otherwise. For that reason, it is an excellent candidate for close reading.

At the middle school level, we tend to share basic forms of poetry with students, starting with the most concrete examples and then moving on to lyric and epic poetry. This example, Carl Sandburg's (1916) "Fog," is a deceptively simple poem. But how far a teacher can ask students to take the poem largely depends on the purpose of the lesson. Because it is short and accessible, teachers often use "Fog" in middle school English language arts classes specifically as an example of lyric poetry. *Lyric poetry* is personal poetry; it focuses on the personal reactions of the poet to the subject. Because lyric poetry is personal, it is often thought of as having a simpler nature than philosophical poetry, but lyric poetry can be as complex as the poet's personal reaction. Sandburg's poem is easy to understand. By the time we encounter Emily Dickinson or John Keats, those personal reactions are complex and highly philosophical.

Here is the complete text of Carl Sandburg's (1916) "Fog":

Fog

The fog comes
on little cat feet.

It sits looking
over harbor and city
on silent haunches
and then moves on.

Six simple lines. Two sentences. In this case, the entire poem is the close reading passage. Let's start with prereading this poem.

Prereading

In developing student readiness to encounter this lyric poem, we can approach the prereading activity in different ways. If we start by studying nature poetry, we might ask students to think about the ways they relate to nature. The teacher could expose students to a natural landscape (either in a picture or video or by taking a walk outside) and ask them for some form of personal reaction—a journal entry, a sketch—any reaction at all. If the focus is more on a study of lyric poetry itself, we might ask students why people write poems. One important answer, and one students nearly always provide, is that the poets are reacting emotionally to some event or experience. We can then ask if the students have a favorite poem, and then take a look at those poems and begin to establish the basic elements of lyric poetry.

Lyric poetry has few basic requirements, but an important one is the poet's emotional reaction. Its form will vary, but we often find lyric poets using figurative language in some way to express that reaction. This observation can lead to a study of some of the basic devices of figurative language (metaphor, simile, personification, and so on). If students provide examples of lyric poems, a quick readiness activity might be to identify these devices in their favorite poems—even without taking much time to analyze their impact. This will raise students' awareness of the basic devices to look for when first reading a lyric poem.

A more thematic approach to prereading for "Fog" would involve the teacher asking students questions that lead to the more important meaning and theme of the poem, such as the following.

• Does nature have meaning in your life?

• Do you think about nature as you are living your everyday life?

This is another way for the teacher to prompt students to begin to think about the relationship humans have with their natural world and how they react to it. Poetry is simply one way human beings have chosen, over the millennia, to express their relationship with nature. Not every teenager sees the value of this form of expression, so perhaps keeping the discussion of the human connection to nature general and then leading to a discussion of poetry as one form that expression takes is a way to prepare students for their first reading of the poem.

It is important, when first encountering lyric poetry, to discuss the students' personal reactions. Invariably, this will be an important part of their initial reading, and teachers should encourage it. A personal connection with the images and words of a poem is one of the reasons we read poetry. At the same time, the purpose of close reading is to move beyond personal reaction to identify and analyze how the poet is creating an effect with the words on the page. So, while personal connections are important, they should only be the focus of the earliest discussion of the poem, and not at the center of most of the work we do on the piece.

Reading Twice and Annotating

We now ask students to read through the poem. Before asking them to do this (especially if this is one of the first encounters with poetry in the class), we may have to do some very basic groundwork about poetry. Students may not understand the structural elements at work in a poem. For example, what is the difference between a paragraph and a stanza? Why are the lines usually set up with the first word capitalized, even though that word does not necessarily start a sentence? And what about rhyme? Aren't all poems supposed to rhyme? What makes a poem a poem?

These are difficult questions, especially for middle school students. Perhaps our best move with students when these questions arise is to focus less on the definitions of poetic form and more on the concept of being open to allowing the poet to develop the form of the writing. Poetry, though it can be highly structured, can also be very loose. That is its great power—it can work in many different ways. Encourage students to not get caught up in the rules of poetry and just watch the poet at work. There will be plenty of time for rules when they get to upper grades and start examining the work of writers like Alexander Pope and William Shakespeare.

The initial reading through these six lines may produce very little. Figure B.1 exemplifies a few things students typically say after their first reading of the poem.

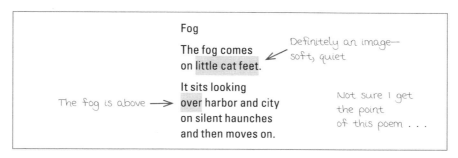

Source: Sandburg, 1916.

Figure B.1: Reading and annotating "Fog."

It isn't much to work with, but this is typical of beginning students encountering what appears to be a very simple poem. They're not sure if there is anything to analyze.

Generating Questions

Occasionally, students do not have much reaction to work with when they generate questions. This is also an important moment to practice; in standardized test situations, students will be on their own. They will want to know what to do if they don't identify much in their initial reading.

We start by asking for their reactions, and then we gauge how well the students did as a class. Most will hold back, unsure of themselves. Teacher modeling helps here. If they haven't come up with much, go back and talk about what kinds of things students should begin to look for. They have probably identified the central image of the poem (the fog as a cat) but may have little else. Imagery is a beginning, but we must now encourage students to pay attention to moments when their thinking is shaken, ever so slightly, by the poem. Modeling that thought process, we might ask students why Sandberg uses certain words: why *comes* in line one, why *little* in line two, why *silent* in line five? Let them consider that for a moment, and then shift the questions. Ask students to be very basic; their curiosity can be a starting point.

The poem is very short, and we can certainly ask *why*. The final comment in the student annotation is, "Not sure I get the point of this poem . . ." Ask students, "Why write something so brief, something that appears to be over before it starts?"

Out of these kinds of conversations (raising questions but not answering them), the teacher prompts students to begin to open up to the larger issues the poem generates. We want students, if they are able at this point, to generate their own analysis questions. But if they are unable, we can suggest some they may adopt. The teacher must be careful here. Let students generate their own questions if they can. The teacher should offer suggestions only if students are unable (not if they are unwilling). Let's suppose the key questions going forward are the following.

- Can such a short poem be an important poem?

- What is important about using the image of the cat to represent fog?

Students can now return to the poem with an eye toward answering these questions as they do a close analytical reading.

Reading Analytically

Even if students have experience close reading prose texts, reading poetry analytically is more challenging for beginning close readers. The format is often distracting, and they have trouble aiming at larger issues, such as the focus questions. For this reason, it is sometimes helpful for students to read for understanding first, comment, and then ask questions. Younger secondary students can benefit by asking them to paraphrase a poem.

Further, beginning student close readers often approach poetry as if each line is a sentence, pausing at the end of each line. This usually creates a problem in understanding and, if not corrected early, creates genuine problems with more complex poetry. Teachers should direct students to read punctuation mark to punctuation mark when they are initially reading for understanding. Model this for them, and they will quickly see the value of it when working with poetry. In applying this method to "Fog," we might get a reading that sounds like the following.

> The fog comes on little cat feet.
> It sits looking over harbor and city on silent haunches and then moves on.

Such a reading eliminates some of the effects of Sandburg's writing, and before we draw any conclusions about the workings of the poem, we would want to encounter the poem in its original form. But when students are trying to understand the poem at a basic level, reading in this way will help them enormously. With a straightforward poem such as "Fog," it may not even be necessary; when students get to more complex poetry, reading punctuation mark to punctuation mark is a lifesaver.

After students have read the poem for understanding and discussed what is going on, send them back for two true analytical readings, with the focus questions in front of them. Ask them to annotate the poem. Figure B.2 shows what some of their responses might be.

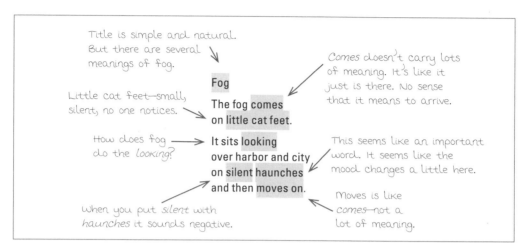

Source: Sandburg, 1916.

Figure B.2: Analytical reading of "Fog."

The two focus questions for this analytical reading are useful as students process through what they've found. One is a very general, thematic question: Can such a short poem be an important poem? The answer to this question may have to wait until students have fully analyzed the poem. The other question creates a better starting point for students to think about their evidence: What is important about using the image of the cat to represent fog? In looking at the notes this student made in figure B.2, there are some initial answers to the question. The cat-like movements of the fog represent the fog effectively, but this student has hit on something that will take that observation further. Consider the comment "*Comes* doesn't carry lots of meaning. It's like it just is there. No sense that it means to arrive." This introduces the idea of intentionality—does the fog intend to enter as it does, and does it have a sense of brooding as it sits on *silent haunches* looking at the city? Though the student doesn't see the issue at this depth, the observation will lead the student to eventually ask that question. We now turn to discussion of the poem.

Discussing as a Class or Analyzing Individually

As the class begins to discuss what students discovered in the analytical readings, students will begin to generate answers to these key questions.

- Can such a short poem be an important poem?

- What is important about using the image of the cat to represent fog?

As previously mentioned, a good place to start is the second question and then see if the class is ready to answer the first, more philosophical question at the end of the analysis. The following figure B.3 (with commentary) imagines the class discussion for this close reading analysis.

Narrative	Commentary
Teacher: You've had the opportunity to read through the poem carefully a couple of times. We have two focus questions, and it would appear that the first one requires that we do some careful discussion of the whole poem before we can answer it. Shall we start with the second question that centers on the image of the cat? What did you notice about that image as you read through the poem carefully?	Setting up the task carefully, but notice the language here. Asks permission. Although it is obvious the class must start on question 2, keep the focus strongly on the group's efforts, rather than teacher direction.
Student 1: It is like the fog is given animal features. It isn't really personification, is it? Is there a name for when the writer gives animal qualities to something that isn't an animal?	Students will focus on the device right away. The term is actually *zoomorphism*, but this isn't the time to focus on the term.
Teacher: There is, but it's a big complicated term that we don't have to worry about right at the moment; we could look that up later. But good point! Animal-like qualities. Anyone want to add to that?	So deflect, but honor that observation.
Student 2: I guess I was asking why the poet chose to use a cat? The poet says it comes on little cat feet, and that would be silent.	Here a student begins to drill down into the image itself. Good move!
Student 3: I thought that too. But why little? Big cat feet would be just as quiet.	A good objection that drives the thinking a little deeper.
Student 1: If they are little, they are even less obvious. I think the poet's saying that the cat sneaks up. The *little* kind of applies to the sound rather than the feet, I think.	This is the right answer, but not all students may see it.
Teacher: What do the rest of you think about that? Is this about describing the sound?	Asking for opinions may uncover objections that will allow the discussion to support the idea further, and that may convince more students.
Student 4: I don't know. If he meant that why wouldn't the poet just say "sounds like little cat feet?"	The discussion goes right where the teacher intends.
Student 1: Well, it's poetry, so sometimes poets just want to say it in fewer words, but they could still mean sound. **Student 5:** I think if we believe the line is about the sound of the fog as silent cat feet, it doesn't really change the meaning much. It could be right.	
Teacher: OK, how about we keep the fact that the opening line describes a sound as a pretty good likelihood and see whether it fits at the end? Other things you found in the poem about the image of the cat?	But now we need to move things along or we will get bogged down in this one issue.
Student 6: I was looking at the second sentence, and I thought something changed when the poet says "silent haunches."	This is a good observation that isn't fully developed.
Teacher: What changed?	Draw the student out.
Student 6: Well, I looked up *haunches*, and it is something about the back leg muscles. So the cat is ready to move—maybe pounce. That sounds like there could be something dangerous.	

Student 3: It seems kind of weird that the poet says "silent haunches." I was thinking about how those two words go together, and I guess if haunches are silent they don't reveal that they are there, and if there is something dangerous going on, if it was silent, then that would be like a threat. So I thought the mood changed.	This student is starting to identify the mood shift in line five. This is a strong observation, because the mood shift is subtle and the poet doesn't fully develop it. A good observation!
Teacher: Anyone else see mood change in the poem? (Some students did, others did not.)	Asking for more evidence.
Teacher: If you saw that change, why would the poet do that? Let's keep focused on the image of the cat, since that is our focus question. Can we ask ourselves why the poet would want to suggest a darker mood in association with the cat?	Placing students in the role of the writer. Not looking for author's intent; rather, suggesting the author is working here and thinking.
Student 7: Cats aren't always furry, purring creatures. They can attack. And they're sly.	Good realistic answer.
Student 8: Yeah, my cat's like that—you can never trust him.	A personal reaction. Important, but off topic.
Student 1: Maybe the poet's trying to suggest something about the fog?	This is the key question about the cat comparison.
Teacher: What might he be trying to suggest?	
Student 7: That like a cat, a fog can be dangerous too.	Bingo.
Student 4: That fits with something else I was thinking about. There are some places in the poem where the cat just does things, and it doesn't seem to think about it. Like the word *comes*—it just comes in, it doesn't seem to think about coming in, and it doesn't do it with a lot of energy.	This comment deepens the understanding of the comparison.
Student 1: That brings up something I was thinking about too. I think the cat does do some things on purpose. It sits there on its silent haunches, and that suggests that it is thinking. But I don't see what it says about fog. Fog doesn't think.	
Teacher: OK, here's a basic question about what the poet's doing in the poem. He chose to use a thinking creature, a cat, as the image of the fog. Now, fog doesn't think, so we have to ask ourselves, "What was the poet thinking about when he did this? What is he saying about the fog?"	Now we have to nail down this interpretation of the cat image. Without this understanding the discussion goes no further.
Student 1: That it kind of thinks. I mean if you're saying it moves and sits like a cat, then it is like the fog means to be there. **Teacher:** What do you think? Is that what the poet is saying? **Student 3:** I guess so. It's poetry so it doesn't have to be real. It is saying something—interpreting about something real. **Teacher:** And what is the poet saying about fog? (Vague answers)	
Teacher: Please turn to someone near you and discuss that question. By using the cat image here, what is the poet suggesting about the fog? (After some student-to-student discussion, the class discussion resumes.)	They need to work through this together.

Figure B.3: A sample narrative with commentary for "Fog."

continued →

Narrative	Commentary
Teacher: Again, what is the poet suggesting about the fog?	Restating the question.
Student 5: That it can be like an animal, dangerous, and silent.	Good response.
Student 3: But also that it is natural and beautiful.	Deepens.
Teacher: So, by using a comparison with a cat, the poet accesses for the fog nearly all the attributes of a cat?	Now, let them object to this overstatement.
Student 1: Well, not all, but some. I mean the fog doesn't go around chasing mice.	Right!
Teacher: Good point! We have to see what the poet wrote about the cat and use those points to see what he is saying about the fog. I think we might have answered our second focus question. Do you have anything further to say about the cat image? (No responses)	Nails down the relationship and cites the fact that we've done good work.
Teacher: Are we ready to take on the first focus question, Can such a short poem be an important poem? (General agreement)	Now we can move to the more philosophical question, because we have the specific evidence for that argument.
Teacher: Let me rephrase the question a bit. What makes a poem an important poem?	Important to define what we mean.
Student 8: It says something more than just a story.	
Teacher: What do you mean by something more?	Drawing student out.
Student 8: Well, it makes a statement. It has a message of some kind.	
Teacher: Do you all agree with that? Do we need to say more? (General agreement)	We can move quickly here; they know the answer.
Teacher: OK, if that is what makes a poem important, is "Fog" an important poem?	Directly state the question.
Student 6: Yes, because it says a lot about fog, more than just it drifts in at night and sits there.	Though they may not realize it, they are identifying theme.
Teacher: What more does it say?	Drawing out.
Student 6: That it is dangerous and sly like a cat.	
Teacher: And now, we've answered the second question, haven't we? Just because a poem is short, it doesn't mean it isn't important. Good job!	Celebrate success!

Using Processing Activities

In a poem as short as this one, processing takes on a different role. Here we have that rare instance where the close reading passage is the entire text, so the important step of placing our close reading analysis within the context of the entire text is unnecessary; we can move students right into processing at a more global level.

Once again, the possibilities for processing are broad. The most obvious next steps are written pieces presenting the analysis of the entire poem, basing the thesis on one or both focus questions. Students should do a good job with this because the poem is accessible and short, and they have identified strong evidence in support of their answers to the focus questions. For these reasons, the poem is a fine opportunity to move into teaching some of the basic elements of persuasive writing, particularly the structure and generation of a thesis statement, the development of a thesis paragraph, the planning and execution of strong supporting paragraphs focused on textual evidence, and that most elusive of skills, the presentation of strong commentary on the evidence.

However, we aren't limited to persuasive writing. "Fog" is an opportunity for creative writing as well, and for the same reasons that it works well with persuasive writing. In studying the development of the poem on a particular natural topic, students are well prepared to model the poem in their own creative writing. Whether that creative writing takes the form of lyric poetry or a short story, the poem can inspire some truly amazing art! Further, students aren't restricted to the written word; their creativity could easily be accessed through artwork or dance.

Literary Example 2

The Adventures of Huckleberry Finn by Mark Twain

Genre: Novel

Grade levels: 10–12

There is a famous quote from novelist Ernest Hemingway: "All modern American literature comes from one book by Mark Twain (1884/1999) called *The Adventures of Huckleberry Finn*" (Culture Shock, n.d.). Scholars have argued this for decades, but Hemingway's comment does suggest the fundamental role of this novel in American literature. Of course, the other side of *The Adventures of Huckleberry Finn* coin is the battle over whether this novel is appropriate in a modern American literature curriculum given its depiction of blatant racism and frequent use of the N-word.

That being said, most American literature teachers would argue that the book is important, and that it should be part of an American high school student's experience. Many teachers who teach the book have to find a way to deal with the racist elements, and usually this is overcome by crediting the fact that the book is a realist work—or one that attempts to depict life as it was at the time, and Twain certainly knew the world of this novel having grown up in Hannibal, Missouri, in the 19th century. Unfortunately, we must admit that racism has been an element of American society from the beginnings of our republic, and most of us would argue that it is still present. Given that context, *The Adventures of Huckleberry Finn*'s role in pointing to the ubiquitous nature of that racism is an important one. But the book is also much more than an examination of racism in 19th century America.

People who like linear theories of literary development will argue with Hemingway that *The Adventures of Huckleberry Finn* (Twain, 1884/1999) is the essential American novel. Prior to Twain's work, there are important American novelists—the first, perhaps, being James Fenimore Cooper.

Cooper's novels depict the beginning of the western movement of America into the frontier, though the frontier of Cooper's novels is western New York State. In the middle of the 19th century, American novelists like Nathaniel Hawthorne and Herman Melville wrote spectacularly important works that identify some of the darker elements of the origins of American society and of the American self, respectively. But it was Twain who took the notion of the *American*—that self-driven outsider who rejected all the influences of the European society the country had rejected as part of the revolution, that youthful, exuberant creature who was most at home in the frontier—and crystalized him in the roguish, plain-thinking, and practical Huckleberry Finn.

In Huck, American readers see themselves as they were in the last quarter of the 19th century, when Twain worked on the novel. Americans were conquerors of the frontier, still working their way west, subduing the land and the native culture to their needs, and rejecting any sense that refined European values would define them. In his journey down the Mississippi River on a raft, Huck represents everything that inspired American adventurism and conquest—a oneness with nature, yet a respect for her power; and a can-do spirit that takes on every challenge and succeeds with a simple, practical approach that rejects philosophy, religion, and the history of European letters in favor of an American natural heroism. It is no accident that the road Huck travels, the Mississippi, is a natural one, and that the dangers of the journey are greatest when Huck leaves the river and engages with society on the shores. Organized society, *sivilization* as Huck calls it, is the enemy. Nature is a place of safety and inspiration for a new nation growing into a continent waiting to be conquered, even in 1886, when the book was published. At the end of the novel, Huck states this eloquently: "But I reckon I got to light out for the Territory ahead of the rest, because aunt Sally she's going to adopt me and sivilize me and I can't stand it. I been there before" (Twain, 1884/1996, p. 296). The Territory, that portion of the continent still devoted to the natural world, is Huck's safest place. The frontier is still open in 1886, and it would remain so in literature until 1926, when F. Scott Fitzgerald declared it closed, guiding American literature away from Horace Greeley's proclamation to "Go West, young man" and focusing American writers on the East in *The Great Gatsby*.

In sharing this novel with American high school students, it is important to place it within that context, one based on the views of American writers in their representation of the growth of the country and of American thought. We can focus on a range of literary issues in the novel, and certainly the representation of racist society in the novel is one of them. But Huck is a picaresque hero, a rogue whom we love, whose development we track across the novel, and who eventually grows, and in doing so, shows the reader the country's own picaresque growth. From that standpoint, the racism of the novel aids in our understanding the vital importance of the growth of Huck, and by implication, of the United States as a nation. At that critical moment in the novel, when Huck rejects everything he has ever been taught about African Americans and decides not to turn in the runaway slave Jim, we can glory in his exclamation, "All right, then, I'll *go* to hell!" (Twain, 1884/1999, p. 223) as a moment of American triumph over racism, however limited that triumph remained in the next century.

Let's be very clear, also, as we ask our young critics to analyze the novel in short close reading passages, that the main character of that same novel would reject such critical reading. Its author states this in a "Notice" before we read even the first word of the novel: "Persons attempting to find a motive in this narrative will be prosecuted; persons attempting to find a moral in it will be banished; persons attempting to find a plot in it will be shot. —BY ORDER OF THE AUTHOR" (Twain, 1884/1999, p. 4). Students always pick up on the obvious irony of our closely reading such a work, but they also catch on quickly that the author put enough into the novel that, by implication, he asked his readers to violate the rules set down in the Notice. But the Notice captures an essential element of the picaresque

American hero—a rejection of anything that requires more than a cursory understanding prior to action. This allows us an important introductory discussion with our students about the changing values Americans have on the issue of intellectualism.

If our focus in the close reading activities for this novel is on the development of the character of Huck Finn, there are many passages that we might choose to close read. For the purposes of this example, we will take a passage which establishes Huck's naturalism and allows us to look at an often-overlooked feature of our practical, no-nonsense American hero—his lyricism. The fact is that when Huck describes his natural surroundings, he very nearly waxes poetic, and this represents a big change from the abrupt and often impulsive reactions he gives in dialogue. The section we will use comes from chapter XIX of the novel, when the Shepherdson and Grangerford episode is over, and Huck and Jim are heading down the river:

> A little smoke couldn't be noticed now, so we would take some fish off of the lines and cook up a hot breakfast. And afterwards we would watch the lonesomeness of the river, and kind of lazy along, and by and by lazy off to sleep. Wake up by and by, and look to see what done it, and maybe see a steamboat coughing along up-stream, so far off towards the other side you couldn't tell nothing about her only whether she was a stern-wheel or side-wheel; then for about an hour there wouldn't be nothing to hear nor nothing to see—just solid lonesomeness. Next you'd see a raft sliding by, away off yonder, and maybe a galoot on it chopping, because they're most always doing it on a raft; you'd see the axe flash and come down—you don't hear nothing; you see that axe go up again, and by the time it's above the man's head then you hear the *k'chunk!*—it had took all that time to come over the water. So we would put in the day, lazying around, listening to the stillness. Once there was a thick fog, and the rafts and things that went by was beating tin pans so the steamboats wouldn't run over them.
>
> A scow or a raft went by so close we could hear them talking and cussing and laughing—heard them plain; but we couldn't see no sign of them; it made you feel crawly; it was like spirits carrying on that way in the air. Jim said he believed it was spirits; but I says:
>
> "No; spirits wouldn't say, 'Dern the dern fog.'"
>
> Soon as it was night out we shoved; when we got her out to about the middle we let her alone, and let her float wherever the current wanted her to; then we lit the pipes, and dangled our legs in the water, and talked about all kinds of things—we was always naked, day and night, whenever the mosquitoes would let us—the new clothes Buck's folks made for me was too good to be comfortable, and besides I didn't go much on clothes, nohow.
>
> Sometimes we'd have that whole river all to ourselves for the longest time. Yonder was the banks and the islands, across the water; and maybe a spark—which was a candle in a cabin window; and sometimes on the water you could see a spark or two—on a raft or a scow, you know; and maybe you could hear a fiddle or a song coming over from one of them crafts. It's lovely to live on a raft. We had the sky up there, all speckled with stars, and we used to lay on our backs and look up at them, and discuss about whether they was made or only just happened. Jim he allowed they was made, but I allowed they happened; I judged it would have took too long to *make* so many. Jim said the moon could a *laid* them; well, that looked kind of reasonable, so I didn't say nothing against it, because I've seen a frog lay most as many, so of course it could be done. We used to watch the stars that fell, too, and see them streak down. Jim allowed they'd got spoiled and was hove out of the nest.
>
> Once or twice of a night we would see a steamboat slipping along in the dark, and now and then she would belch a whole world of sparks up out of her chimbleys, and they would rain down in the river and look awful pretty; then she would turn a corner and her lights would wink out and her powwow shut off and leave the river still again; and by and by her waves would get to us, a long

time after she was gone, and joggle the raft a bit, and after that you wouldn't hear nothing for you couldn't tell how long, except maybe frogs or something.

After midnight the people on shore went to bed, and then for two or three hours the shores was black—no more sparks in the cabin windows. These sparks was our clock—the first one that showed again meant morning was coming, so we hunted a place to hide and tie up right away. (Twain, 1884/1999, pp. 136–137)

Prereading

Whenever we approach a full-length work with our students, we encounter the problem of whether to prepare students to read the entire novel or just the section they will close read. Assuming our students will read the entire novel at some point, whether before or after close reading our selection, we will prepare them for this larger engagement with the entire work in any number of common ways, raising their interest in particular thematic issues in the novel. For the purposes of our selection, let's look at prereading activities tied directly to this passage.

First, we must settle on a focus for this passage. As previously stated, one focus can be the lyricism of the novel's narrator (Huck), as exemplified in this selection. If this is our focus, our prereading activities should assess students' thoughts on the issue of lyricism in narrative writing. Thus, students must understand what lyrical writing is. If they are students in tenth to twelfth grade, they will have encountered lyrical writing as poetry in several previous classes. They may not understand what lyrical writing is in a narrative, nor may they understand how to identify the methods an author uses to create lyrical writing. While the selected passage is chosen as an opportunity for them to analyze such writing, they will need the background knowledge not only of what lyrical narrative writing is but also how an author creates that writing. We will assume that there will be some instruction in the *how* of lyrical writing prior to the close reading lessons that follow, but we might start by having students identify what lyrical writing is.

Let's begin by refining our own understanding of this term. According to William Harman and C. Hugh Holman (2003), a *lyrical novel* is "a species of novel in which conventional narration is subordinated to the presentation of inner thoughts, feelings and moods." According to Ralph Freedman (as cited in Harmon & Holman, 2003), the *lyrical novel* transforms "the materials of fiction (such as characters, plots, or scenes) into patterns of imagery" (p. 293). No one would claim that *The Adventures of Huckleberry Finn* is a lyrical novel, but the definition is a useful starting point for understanding the elements at work in the lyrical sections of Huck's narration.

In discussing Huck as narrator, we engage all the issues of realist writing. Huck is not well educated and speaks in a colloquial manner; this is purposeful on Twain's part—we as readers need to understand the relevancy of Huck's words. The novel is told in first person by a reliable but uneducated narrator. The book opens with lines that establish the characteristics of Huck's narration:

You don't know about me, without you have read a book by the name of *The Adventures of Tom Sawyer*; but that ain't no matter. That book was made by Mr. Mark Twain, and he told the truth, mainly. There was things which he stretched, but mainly he told the truth. That is nothing. I never seen anybody but lied one time or another, without it was Aunt Polly, or the widow, or maybe Mary. Aunt Polly—Tom's Aunt Polly, she is—and Mary, and the Widow Douglas is all told about in that book, which is mostly a true book, with some stretchers, as I said before. (Twain, 1884/1999, p. 13)

Students will often immediately identify Huck's dialect as uneducated as they read these opening lines, and the reasons are easy to identify—the use of *ain't* and the substitution of *without* for *unless* in the first sentence, as well as the lack of subject-verb agreement. Also, the passage is poorly organized, starting off by discussing Huck's own history in the previous novel and wandering off to a discussion of the frequency of lying. Huck establishes a narrative voice here, and that voice clearly creates an understanding between reader and narrator about the kind of reasoning the narrator will exhibit as the story proceeds. We should point out the highly effective nature of Twain's establishing a narrative voice in the beginning of this book; those in the 19th century who wished to ban the book from public libraries voiced that as one of their primary objections to the novel.

Throughout most of the book, we see this narrative voice as consistent with the character established in these opening lines. Huck takes a very practical approach to any form of reasoning, as when, in our passage, Jim suggests that the stars, being so many, must have been "birthed" by the moon, to which Huck responds with "well, that looked kind of reasonable, so I didn't say nothing against it, because I've seen a frog lay most as many, so of course it could be done." He also shares much of his own thoughts and feelings with the reader throughout the novel, the most important example being his decision not to turn in Jim as a runaway slave, as mentioned previously. Further, Huck is limited in his descriptive powers in some places in the novel by seeing towns and the people in them in restricted terms. But his narration is decidedly different when he comes to describe natural scenes, and it is this difference in narration that we wish to have our students analyze.

An element of lyricism enters the description when the narrator shifts from literal to figurative description. While such figurative language remains within the confines of the characterization Twain establishes for Huck, the narrator begins to use comparison and imagery. In doing this, Twain shows the reader the depths of Huck's reasoning ability; figurative language is not something we associate with someone of limited thinking. Huck is far from that, even if he is uneducated in the conventional sense. To a certain extent, this is Twain commenting on American potential—though the American population may have been largely uneducated in the middle of the 19th century, Americans are far from poorly equipped for the challenges of establishing a new society in an unexplored continent.

So, as we prepare our students to engage with this kind of writing, we might begin by presenting students with a sample description that includes imagery and figurative language, asking first for their reactions to it, and then asking them to rewrite the description without the imagery and figurative language. For example, the following is a short passage from Wharton's (1911/1992) novel *Ethan Frome* in which her narrator describes Starkfield, Massachusetts, one of the settings of the novel:

> The village lay under two feet of snow with drifts at the windy corners. In a sky of iron the points of the Dipper hung like icicles and Orion flashed his cold fires. The moon had set, but the night was so transparent that the white house-fronts between the elms looked gray against the snow, clumps of bushes made black stains on it, and the basement windows of the church sent shafts of yellow light far across the endless undulations. (p. 12)

This short passage is a good starting point for discussing the *how* of developing narrative lyricism, and its tone is substantially different than the passage from *The Adventures of Huckleberry Finn*.

Reading Twice and Annotating

Our students now turn to the passage from *The Adventures of Huckleberry Finn* with the focus on the language of the passage. We remind students to think carefully not only about *what* Twain is doing in the passage but also *how* he is doing it. Figure B.4 (pages 120–121) shows how one student might annotate the passage.

Starts with a very factual statement.

A little smoke couldn't be noticed now, so we would take some fish off of the lines and cook up a hot breakfast. And afterwards we would watch the lonesomeness of the river, and kind of lazy along, and by and by lazy off to

Made up word? Uses lazy as a verb.

Repetition

sleep. Wake up by and by, and look to see what done it, and maybe see a steamboat coughing along up-stream, so far off towards the other side you couldn't tell nothing about her only whether she was a stern-wheel or side-

Not clear whether he means this word positively or negatively.

wheel; then for about an hour there wouldn't be nothing to hear nor nothing to see—just solid lonesomeness. Next you'd see a raft sliding by, away off yonder, and maybe a galoot on it chopping, because they're most always doing it on a raft; you'd see the axe flash and come down—you don't hear

You get the feeling this is a real event he is reporting. The experience is real.

nothing; you see that axe go up again, and by the time it's above the man's head then you hear the *k'chunk!*—it had took all that time to come over the

How do you listen to stillness?

water. So we would put in the day, lazying around, listening to the stillness. Once there was a thick fog, and the rafts and things that went by was beating tin pans so the steamboats wouldn't run over them.

A scow or a raft went by so close we could hear them talking and cussing and laughing—heard them plain; but we couldn't see no sign of them; it made

Personal reaction—lyrical

you feel crawly; it was like spirits carrying on that way in the air. Jim said he

simile

believed it was spirits; but I says:

"No; spirits wouldn't say, 'Dern the dern fog.'"   *Right back to a practical reaction!*

Soon as it was night out we shoved; when we got her out to about the middle we let her alone, and let her float wherever the current wanted her to; then

Sense of freedom here.

we lit the pipes, and dangled our legs in the water, and talked about all kinds of things—we was always naked, day and night, whenever the mosquitoes would let us—the new clothes Buck's folks made for me was too good to be comfortable, and besides I didn't go much on clothes, nohow.

The sentence before this supports this statement. But the words he uses aren't what you expect from a young boy. He really does appreciate how nice the life is on a raft.

Sometimes we'd have that whole river all to ourselves for the longest time. Yonder was the banks and the islands, across the water; and maybe a spark—which was a candle in a cabin window; and sometimes on the water you could see a spark or two—on a raft or a scow, you know; and maybe you could hear a fiddle or a song coming over from one of them crafts. It's lovely to live on a raft. We had the sky up there, all speckled with stars, and we used to lay on our backs and look up at them, and discuss about whether they was made or only just happened. Jim he allowed they was made, but I allowed

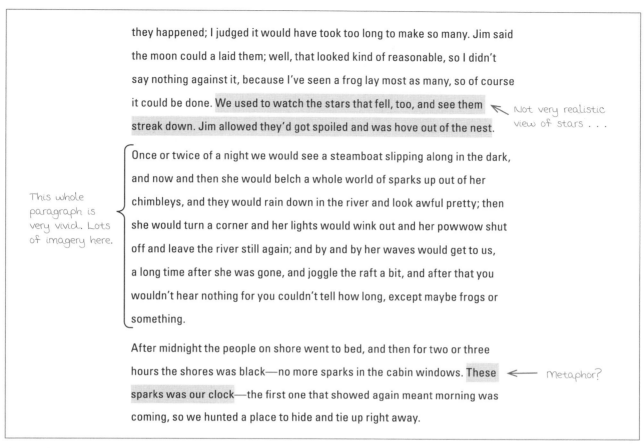

they happened; I judged it would have took too long to make so many. Jim said the moon could a laid them; well, that looked kind of reasonable, so I didn't say nothing against it, because I've seen a frog lay most as many, so of course it could be done. We used to watch the stars that fell, too, and see them streak down. Jim allowed they'd got spoiled and was hove out of the nest.

Not very realistic view of stars . . .

Once or twice of a night we would see a steamboat slipping along in the dark, and now and then she would belch a whole world of sparks up out of her chimbleys, and they would rain down in the river and look awful pretty; then she would turn a corner and her lights would wink out and her powwow shut off and leave the river still again; and by and by her waves would get to us, a long time after she was gone, and joggle the raft a bit, and after that you wouldn't hear nothing for you couldn't tell how long, except maybe frogs or something.

This whole paragraph is very vivid. Lots of imagery here.

After midnight the people on shore went to bed, and then for two or three hours the shores was black—no more sparks in the cabin windows. These sparks was our clock—the first one that showed again meant morning was coming, so we hunted a place to hide and tie up right away.

metaphor?

Source: Twain, 1884/1999, pp. 136–137.

Figure B.4: Reading and annotating *The Adventures of Huckleberry Finn*.

It's interesting to note the limited student response on the first couple of readings of this passage. This student is seeing some important things, but many areas of the passage are annotated in a very general way (see figure B.4). This is typical of a high school student's interaction with Twain's writing. The writing appears so straightforward that little pops out at first. But a great deal is going on here, and we're going to have to establish that in our initial discussion with the students concerning their reading twice and annotating.

Generating Questions

The passage selected for close reading from *The Adventures of Huckleberry Finn* suggests one of the most common questions about close reading: What is the purpose of close reading? Is the idea to unpack the thematic elements of the text, or are we focused on analyzing whatever the author is doing in the selected texts? In this passage, theme is not the primary focus. So, we might answer these two questions simply by saying we should concentrate on analyzing the textual elements, whatever they may be. In narrowing the students' focus in this manner, we equip them with the ability to see whatever is in the text, no matter what the text is, and this is important preparation for standardized tests and adult reading. But we should also note that in focusing on textual analysis, we are taking the first step in focusing on theme. With a writer of Twain's quality, virtually nothing in the novel will be placed there gratuitously. Eventually, everything will connect in some way with the theme, although, as in our passage, it may not be apparent.

In a discussion after the initial readings and annotation of this passage, the class might find it doesn't quite know which questions to ask. There will be many observations about the colloquial nature of Huck and Jim's dialogue, but at this point in the novel that will be nothing new. Some students will likely observe that Huck appreciates the natural world he is encountering, but that is also something that good readers will have observed prior to chapter XIX. For example, much the same kind of writing can be found in a brief section of chapter VII:

> I got out amongst the driftwood, and then laid down in the bottom of the canoe and let her float. I laid there, and had a good rest and a smoke out of my pipe, looking away into the sky; not a cloud in it. The sky looks ever so deep when you lay down on your back in the moonshine; I never knowed it before. And how far a body can hear on the water such nights! I heard people talking at the ferry landing. I heard what they said, too—every word of it. (Twain, 1884/1999, p. 47)

In terms of style, there is a great similarity between these few lines and the passage our students are working on. So, the question is not one of characterization, particularly, although our work will add to our understanding of Huck as a character. The key questions to ask with our passage center around authorial choices.

1. Why is there a shift in Huck's reaction to events he is encountering from one of pure practicality to one of romantic engagement in the natural world?

2. Just how does Twain accomplish this shift?

In other words, what is happening in the text that signals to the reader that a shift has occurred?

It is unlikely, though possible, that high school students will generate questions at this level or in these words. When we have a passage that doesn't, at the surface, present obvious issues that a high school reader might identify for further investigation, we need to draw students deeper into the text to generate those questions. Although we can provide the questions to the students, it is better if they generate them on their own, or at least with our guidance. When the teacher provides, orally or in writing, a series of discussion questions, this can lead to students creating such textual analysis questions. We might ask the following.

• "Do you see any shift in the way Huck thinks in this passage?" (A question of *what* the author is doing)

• "How would you describe that shift—from what to what?" (A question of *what* the author is doing)

• "Why would Twain present such a shift in this narrative event?" (A question of *why* the author is doing something)

From the class discussion of these questions, it is likely the class would create the following textual analysis questions.

• Why does Twain show Huck being very practical when he talks to Jim and then being very descriptive, maybe even emotional, in his thinking?

• How does Twain create the shift described in question 1?

With those close analysis questions in hand, we ask students to return to the text and read it, repeatedly and closely.

Reading Analytically

The process here, as in our other examples, is slow and deliberate. Be sure to offer plenty of time for students to read several times and do the proper annotations before proceeding. Figure B.5 depicts our student's additional annotations to her first remarks, keeping the two focus questions in mind. (Again, this figure shows only the new observations.)

This sentence shows a change from the factual nature of the first sentence, and the sentence reports something Huck is thinking, so even here Twain is showing a difference when Huck is thinking versus when he speaks to Jim.

A little smoke couldn't be noticed now, so we would take some fish off of the lines and cook up a hot breakfast. And afterwards we would watch the lonesomeness of the river, and kind of lazy along, and by and by lazy off to sleep. Wake up by and by, and look to see what done it, and maybe see a steamboat coughing along up-stream, so far off towards the other side you couldn't tell nothing about her only whether she was a stern-wheel or side-wheel; then for about an hour there wouldn't be nothing to hear nor nothing to see—just solid lonesomeness. Next you'd see a raft sliding by, away off yonder, and maybe a galoot on it chopping, because they're most always doing it on a raft; you'd see the axe flash and come down—you don't hear nothing; you see that axe go up again, and by the time it's above the man's head then you hear the *k'chunk!*—it had took all that time to come over the water. So we would put in the day, lazying around, listening to the stillness. Once there was a thick fog, and the rafts and things that went by was beating tin pans so the steamboats wouldn't run over them.

The third sentence goes back to mostly factual reporting.

Interesting sentence—factual reporting, but the word choice shows some of the description Huck does when thinking.

Here's a place where we can see the contrast between the two forms of Huck's character.

A scow or a raft went by so close we could hear them talking and cussing and laughing—heard them plain; but we couldn't see no sign of them; it made you feel crawly; it was like spirits carrying on that way in the air. Jim said he believed it was spirits; but I says:

"No; spirits wouldn't say, 'Dern the dern fog.'"

All of this is simple description, but everything is focused on showing how free they felt on the river. Good description.

Thinking about the shift we are looking for, this sentence totally sets up the next short one. This sentence is long, with lots of complications, and it shows the contrast between life on the river and life on the shore.

Soon as it was night out we shoved; when we got her out to about the middle we let her alone, and let her float wherever the current wanted her to; then we lit the pipes, and dangled our legs in the water, and talked about all kinds of things—we was always naked, day and night, whenever the mosquitoes would let us—the new clothes Buck's folks made for me was too good to be comfortable, and besides I didn't go much on clothes, nohow.

The thinking here is the way Huck usually interacts with others—very commonsense and connected with his life experience.

Sometimes we'd have that whole river all to ourselves for the longest time. Yonder was the banks and the islands, across the water; and maybe a spark—which was a candle in a cabin window; and sometimes on the water you could see a spark or two—on a raft or a scow, you know; and maybe you could hear a fiddle or a song coming over from one of them crafts. It's lovely to live on a raft. We had the sky up there, all speckled with stars, and we used to lay on our backs and look up at them, and discuss about whether they was made or only just happened. Jim he allowed they was made, but I allowed they happened; I judged it would have took too long to make so many. Jim said

The first part of this sentence is more emotionally descriptive, and then Twain is heading back to telling a specific factual incident, so it shifts back.

Figure B.5: Analytical reading of *The Adventures of Huckleberry Finn.*

continued →

the moon could a laid them; well, that looked kind of reasonable, so I didn't

say nothing against it, because I've seen a frog lay most as many, so of course

it could be done. We used to watch the stars that fell, too, and see them

streak down. Jim allowed they'd got spoiled and was hove out of the nest.

Once or twice of a night we would see a steamboat slipping along in the dark,   *Descriptive verbs*

and now and then she would belch a whole world of sparks up out of her

chimbleys, and they would rain down in the river and look awful pretty; then

Interesting image. she would turn a corner and her lights would wink out and her powwow shut   *Not sure what*
It is reporting *this word means.*
something Huck off and leave the river still again; and by and by her waves would get to us,
has experienced
himself, but in a a long time after she was gone, and joggle the raft a bit, and after that you
way that makes
you think—about wouldn't hear nothing for you couldn't tell how long, except maybe frogs or
how things change
back to nature something.
after something
man-made After midnight the people on shore went to bed, and then for two or three   *The sparks are*
interrupts nature. *evidence of people*
Very gradual. hours the shores was black—no more sparks in the cabin windows. These   *and society. When*
they are not
sparks was our clock—the first one that showed again meant morning was   *present, the shore is*
just black—a blank.
coming, so we hunted a place to hide and tie up right away.

Source: Twain, 1884/1999, pp. 136–137.

These further reactions focus on the shift the students are tracking, but they are not deep observations, and, with only a few exceptions, they do not identify specific literary devices at work in the text. To answer the second question, we will need to have students interpret the text in terms of literary devices, so that will be a necessary focus of class discussion.

Discussing as a Class

We now proceed with a class discussion of the students' annotations as follows in figure B.6.

Narrative	Commentary
Teacher: As we start discussing this passage, let's turn to our two focus questions on the board— Why does Twain show Huck being very practical when he talks to Jim and then being very descriptive, maybe even emotional, in his thinking? How does Twain create the shift described in question 1? Anyone want to start us with an observation about either of these questions?	As always, we start by framing the discussion around the focus questions.
Student 1: This passage is difficult. I mean, there's a lot here in Huck's words, but the changes we were talking about in those questions are hard to see. But I found one moment where it seems pretty obvious that Huck	

shifts from the way he talks to the way he thinks. It's actually the whole second paragraph: "A scow or a raft went by so close we could hear them talking and cussing and laughing—heard them plain; but we couldn't see no sign of them; it made you feel crawly; it was like spirits carrying on that way in the air. Jim said he believed it was spirits; but I says: "No; spirits wouldn't say, 'Dern the dern fog.'"	This student is likely expressing the frustrations of many. It is not an easy passage for these focus questions. It's important to get this frustration in public. At least this student goes on to start the discussion with an example.
In the first part of the paragraph, that is all one sentence, he uses a simile—"like spirits carrying on that way in the air." But when he discusses the same thing with Jim, he says something very logical, very practical—"spirits wouldn't say 'Dern the dern fog.'"	Notes syntax issue and completely ignores it! This student focuses on the easier device—a simile.
Teacher: Anyone like to comment on that particular portion of the passage? (No comments)	
Teacher: It does seem like we have a good example of the difference in the text that our questions ask about. So, what we have on the table right now is that when Huck is thinking, he uses a literary device like a simile, but when he speaks, he doesn't.	Restating what we have. Clarifying the current question. Trying not to add anything.
Student 2: Yes, that is true in this case. But he doesn't do that much elsewhere in the passage. I didn't find another simile.	Very correct. This won't go very far.
Student 3: I think that's right. But it is true that the language is different when Huck is thinking than when he speaks. He just doesn't always use similes.	This is a slightly different issue. This student has taken something of a dead end and broadened it into something that can develop.
Teacher: OK, that is important. So, our task now is to broaden our hypothesis about just how Twain shows this shift. We originally thought it was built on similes, but we know you can't really generalize like that, especially if we can't find other instances of that device. So our hypothesis is too narrow.	Teacher nails that down.
Student 4: He does use different diction when he thinks.	The diction discussion must happen but won't be productive. But students need to say it and solve that problem.
Teacher: OK, what do you mean? How is the diction different?	
Student 4: Well, when he speaks to Jim, we said he's very practical. He uses simple words—"spirits wouldn't say . . ." There is nothing in there that needs interpretation. It just means what he says. But when he thinks, the words are more descriptive. For example, "These sparks was our clock." There is no way that sparks are actually a clock. He means that we used them as if they were a clock; that they could in some way tell time from them. So that sentence is kind of like a metaphor.	The discussion shifts from diction to metaphor. The question raised here is subtle yet important.
Student 5: But does he mean it metaphorically when he says, "These sparks was our clock"? I mean, does he mean to say that the sparks were the clock or that the sparks had clock-like qualities?	Student is not explaining this well, but she has a valid point. Is the use of metaphor for poetic effect or just clarification?

Figure B.6: A class discussion of the students' annotations for *The Adventures of Huckleberry Finn*.

continued →

Narrative	Commentary
Student 4: What is the difference? **Student 5:** I'm not sure I can explain it. Uh, you know when a poet uses a metaphor he says something is something else to show the relationship between those two things and that has some meaning for the poem that he intends. When Huck says, "These sparks was our clock" he is just saying we used the sparks like a clock. Do you get what I'm saying? **Student 4:** Yeah, I guess. Huck is just saying they used the sparks like a clock. But, I guess my point was that thinking that is different than the way he talks. That it isn't straightforward, like he talks.	
Teacher: So, what we're saying is, that in the case of this metaphor, we have an example of Huck's different way of thinking, but that it isn't as deliberately poetic (or lyrical, we might say) as if he were a poet describing the same thing. Can we say any more about that?	Honoring this question and clarifying. Also moving past it.
Student 6: Huck isn't very educated, so I don't think I would expect him, in his mind, to be really deeply poetic. This seems like it is a pretty big shift from the way he talks. So, if he thinks this way, why doesn't he talk this way?	What a great question, but too early to answer it.
Teacher: That is a very interesting question. Before we answer it, and it will be very important to answer it, let's get a little more evidence of the qualities of Huck's narration as he is thinking. We've identified a simile and a metaphor. We started down the diction road but got, rightly, sidetracked into the metaphor discussion. Can we identify some other diction that is typical of Huck's narration of his thinking? Please turn to your discussion partners and share your evidence of diction. (Some time for working in small groups) **Teacher:** OK, any examples of diction from the sections where Huck is thinking?	Let's deal with diction. It is the easy device students light on first, but in this passage, there isn't much to glean. That needs to be established.
Student 7: He uses *lonesomeness* a lot. **Student 8:** Is that a real word? **Teacher:** Well, there is certainly an easy way to find out. Phones out! (After some word searching) **Student 8:** It is a real word, but not used very much. *Loneliness* is preferred. **Teacher:** OK, so we have Huck using a word that is kind of rare, but wouldn't really be unusual for someone of his background, wouldn't you agree? (General agreement) Any other diction evidence? **Student 9:** At one point he says, "it made you feel crawly." *Crawly* is pretty descriptive.	Pretty thin evidence. Fact is, Huck thinks in the same words in which he speaks. Consistent characterization on Twain's part, but not much help for our discussion.
Student 3: I have to say, I kept looking at diction words in this passage, and there are a few—*belch, crawly*—but there aren't many. I didn't see much difference in the words he was using when he was telling the story and when he was speaking. (General agreement—to the point of frustration)	Good that a student makes this observation. Gives the teacher some permission to move on. But to what? Students are at a roadblock, so it is time to remind them how to move around a roadblock.

Teacher: So you're saying that diction doesn't tell us much about Twain's technique? **Student 5:** Yes. That is why this passage is so hard for the questions we have! (General agreement)	
Teacher: OK, let me understand where we are. We have found a couple of literary devices, and we have found next to no diction evidence. And we don't have an answer to how Twain is creating a different style for Huck's thinking than when he speaks. (Pause) And we have no additional ideas about Twain's method in the passage? (No response) OK, let me remind you of our process. When one tool, like diction, doesn't work, we need another tool, don't we? Now let's go back and look at our questions. Why does Twain show Huck being very practical when he talks to Jim and then being very descriptive, maybe even emotional, in his thinking? How does Twain create the shift described in question 1?	Modeling and explaining the kind of thinking they should do on their own—particularly in a testing situation.
Try restating our task in terms of literary analysis. Another way of saying question 2 would be, How does Twain create the shift in tone described in question 1? Is that a correct restatement? Isn't the shift one of tone? I mean, isn't that what we've been struggling with? (General agreement) OK, you know where I'm going, don't you? What are the elements of tone? Diction is just one. What are the others?	They need to see that the questions ask about a difference in style and tone. Getting to tone allows them to get around the diction roadblock.
Student 1: Language, details. **Student 5:** Imagery and syntax.	Yup!
Teacher: Yes! So, if diction doesn't work, perhaps one or more of these others will. So, back into small groups, and let's focus on any or all of the other elements of tone—imagery, details, language, and syntax. (Some time to work in small groups) **Teacher:** OK, after some time working through those devices, where are we?	Keep the enthusiasm up. We have a potential way forward. Let's explore!
Student 2: Syntax worked really well. When Huck speaks, he says things in short sentences, but when he thinks, he thinks in long, complicated sentences. I mean, his ideas aren't that complicated, but the sentences go on and on, sometimes a whole paragraph like in paragraph two.	Surprisingly, students go first to the most challenging device—syntax. And in this passage it will tell us a lot.
Student 6: We saw that too. We were looking at the start of paragraph four— "Sometimes we'd have that whole river all to ourselves for the longest time. Yonder was the banks and the islands, across the water; and maybe a spark—which was a candle in a cabin window; and sometimes on the water you could see a spark or two—on a raft or a scow, you know; and maybe you could hear a fiddle or a song coming over from one of them crafts. It's lovely to live on a raft. We had the sky up there, all speckled with stars, and we used to lay on our backs and look up at them, and discuss about whether they was made or only just happened."	Good sample to look at for syntax.

continued →

Narrative	Commentary
Student 7: The second sentence is really long and complicated because he is describing something complicated—the way light and sound move across distance. And then he has a really short sentence: "It's lovely to live on a raft." And that sentence kind of summarizes his point in the section, and he does it by changing the syntax, going with a short sentence, so the reader really notices it.	Note that the student makes an observation and draws a conclusion. Good work.
Student 9: We were talking about that paragraph too and that sentence about "lovely to live on a raft." There is something going on there with language—*lovely* isn't a word you expect from a young boy. But it seems just right for the way Huck is describing things. It kind of surprises the reader, because it is really descriptive and not something you expect.	Important follow-up to the previous comment. Students are beginning to get some momentum in linking evidence to the author's method.
Student 7: And in that long second sentence, there is an interrupting passage—"which was a candle in a cabin window; and sometimes on the water you could see a spark or two." So, the syntax is even more complicated, but the way he interrupts makes sense for a young boy, because he is just clarifying what he is saying. And that is the way a person would think. You don't always think in complete evenly flowing sentences. **Teacher:** OK, so we're saying that the syntax in these sections tends to be more complex. By that, I don't mean that it always consists of long sentences but that it reflects the way people think—sometimes long, complicated sentences, sometimes short, pithy statements. What about the syntax when he is speaking? What is our evidence there? **Student 3:** Well, we really only have the one statement, about the spirits not saying, "Dern the dern fog." But the sentences are short. **Student 6:** He says he told Jim "but I allowed they happened" when they are talking about the stars. It isn't dialogue, but it indicates a pretty straightforward statement, so that might be some more evidence.	Interesting interpretation, linking syntax and characterization. This is good work!
Teacher: OK, we have good evidence of a difference in syntax. How about other elements of tone?	Looking to move past syntax.
Student 8: There are lots of moments where he uses imagery when he is thinking. I think the first one is in the second sentence, "And afterwards we would watch the lonesomeness of the river, and kind of lazy along, and by and by lazy off to sleep." We're back to that word *lonesomeness*, but it goes a long way to helping the reader see what Huck and Jim were watching. It really captures the quiet and the fact that they are alone. And that becomes a big deal as the description goes on. And also, when he says they "lazy along," I mean, I've never heard of the word *lazy* used as a verb. But here it is, and it works!	Imagery is a big one in this passage, and we have finally gotten there!
Student 1: That paragraph keeps right on going with the imagery. When he says, "maybe see a steamboat coughing along up-stream," you have to talk about the verb *coughing*. It's a diction choice, but it really is an imagery issue, because it not only creates a sound but it creates a picture. Really the right word to take you to where Huck is on the river.	Good observation. Firm understanding of how imagery works.

Student 10: And when he is starting the section on the stars, he says, "We had the sky up there, all speckled with stars, and we used to lay on our backs and look up at them, and discuss about whether they was made or only just happened." That is a really interesting image, "speckled with stars," because they go on to talk about whether the stars were laid like a fish lays eggs, and fish are speckled.	And the imagery evidence just begins to flow . . .
Student 4: We are finding tons of images in this passage.	
Teacher: Well, what conclusion can we draw? Let's return to the questions. Why does Twain show Huck being very practical when he talks to Jim and then being very descriptive, maybe even emotional, in his thinking? How does Twain create the shift described in question 1? Perhaps we can best answer the second one first.	Time to shut this off. It is obvious we could keep right on going, but we have enough to move to conclusion. Back to the questions.
Student 7: Big differences in imagery and syntax.	Answer to the second question is now easy.
Teacher: Definitely! Now, what about the first question. Any ideas? (Not much response) OK, we've been really focused on the how question, the second one. Take a moment in your groups and discuss the why question, the first one. (Some time for small group discussion) **Teacher:** OK, after some group discussion, what are your thoughts about question 1?	They need time to process this question after reaching a conclusion on the second question.
Student 2: It could be that Huck is a very different kind of person inside than outside. **Student 5:** Yeah, we thought that like everyone, he doesn't talk the way he thinks. I mean, you don't say everything you think.	
Student 9: And when he speaks in this passage, he is speaking to Jim. So maybe he has a certain way of speaking to Jim that is different than the way he thinks.	An important observation—different audiences, Jim and himself.
Teacher: Do you have a different way of speaking aloud than the way you internally think? (General agreement)	Generalize and personalize the question.
Teacher: The important question is, Why? Why do you have a different way of speaking than thinking?	The key question. Answer this and we have a conclusion!
Student 4: Because we don't always share every bit of ourselves with others.	
Teacher: Do you agree? (General agreement) And I think that is quite normal. So Huck thinks one way, but chooses how much he shares with others, just like anyone else. So although he appears kind of practical and a bit backward to others . . .	Offering students the opportunity for the conclusion.

continued →

Narrative	Commentary
Student 3: He is actually a pretty deep thinker.	
Teacher: Yes. So we can perhaps now answer the question—why would Twain show Huck this way?	Back to the novel and theme.
Student 6: To show that Huck is human.	Not a deep enough answer.
Teacher: That is certainly true, but think of Twain working away on this particular character in this particular book. Why might he show the difference between the internal and the external Huck?	Honor the response but go deeper.
Student 7: Because Huck represents America at the time. We might seem a little backward, but there's more there than you can tell. **Teacher:** Right on.	Bingo.

We could certainly ask students to take this discussion further. With the conclusions reached in this discussion, we can begin to place this passage in the larger context of the novel up to the point of this section, or of the entire work if students have read the entire novel and are returning to close read certain passages. It is a short journey from this discussion to a study of character and theme in the book.

Using Processing Activities

As with our entire lesson for this passage, to make good decisions about the final stage of our process we must understand the objective—a focus on just this passage or on the entire novel and the passage's role in the larger work. Either works; but the activity at the end should align with our original objective.

Since our objective in this sample focused on the passage as a stand-alone piece, we start there in generating a processing activity. Still, one of the important issues in close reading is the applicability of the information and the hypothesis we are testing in terms of larger issues at work in the text. We will find that, inevitably, students will work toward a larger meaning beyond the text. We should encourage this. After all, it is the reason we do close reading.

For this passage, we could begin with a final discussion that focuses on establishing meaning for our uncovered evidence. We might refer to this as a *so what?* discussion. If we have drilled down deeply into the text and discovered, in this case, that Twain is actively presenting an internal Huck and an external Huck, that is all well and good, but what can we say about that?

In such a discussion, we might start by asking students to establish categories of issues in the literary analysis of the novel that potentially fit our hypothesis. For example, the fact that we have two Hucks in this passage might have thematic implications. It would also likely have characterization implications. Ask students to brainstorm potential categories, then divide them into groups to use the information established in the previous class's discussion to investigate whether the hypothesis can be applied to each category. Each group might then present its evidence and conclusions, and the class can then draw larger conclusions.

We will ask students to do some final processing on a larger scale, in any number of ways, but this first step of applying the hypothesis to larger analytical issues in the work is important because students do not always automatically see the relevance of work at the micro level. They can get lost in the minutia, and pulling the lens out to the macro view enables them to take on a task such as writing a paper presenting the hypothesis and evidence. Of course, there are many ways to process this passage other than a paper. We might ask students to rewrite the passage into dialogue that hints at the internal Huck by changing the way he speaks, and then ask them to analyze the difference between what they wrote and the way Twain wrote the passage. Students could also stage a brief scene of such a dialogue for the entire class.

Another technique is to introduce an acting concept to students. Many actors work with a text through a process often referred to as *subtext*. In a play, the *subtext* is what is happening inside the character's head that is not necessarily coming out in the spoken words of the dialogue. Classically, this activity is done with four actors, two speaking the dialogue lines of the play and two others standing behind the speaking actors and whispering the subtext. It can be very revealing of the characters' motivations and thoughts, and this is an important issue for actors to understand if they are to present a rich characterization in a performance. Of course, *The Adventures of Huckleberry Finn* is not a play, but present in our passage is evidence of an external, speaking Huck and an internal, thinking Huck. After introducing the concept of subtext, we might ask students to return to evidence of the thinking Huck in the passage and identify the subtext. A discussion of this work would highlight not only the literary devices already identified in the passage but also the ways in which those literary devices support the subtext.

Informational Example

Pericles's Funeral Oration (from *History of the Peloponnesian War* by Thucydides)

Genre: Informational text

Grade levels: 9–10

As an example of pure rhetorical excellence, there are few more classic examples than Pericles's Funeral Oration from Thucydides's *History of the Peloponnesian War*. Teachers often use this text in world literature classes, but it is also a primary-source document appropriate for world history classes. Teachers would use this text most likely for ninth or tenth grade, but world literature and history are taught at various grade levels in different school systems. Students at this level should be familiar with some aspects of rhetorical analysis.

From a historical standpoint, two Greek historians, Herodotus and Thucydides, are usually identified as the first writers of extensive histories. Indeed, Herodotus is often referred to as the father of history and is best known for his *Histories*, a work that describes the war between the Greek city-states and the Persian Empire. Herodotus is famous for his love of storytelling and those discursive moments of description and relating of tales that sometimes move the text far away from what we might think of as modern history. Thucydides, while far from a modern historian, makes an attempt to relate the details of the events he describes with some degree of historical accuracy and is focused on the character and psychology of the major figures he describes. His relation of Pericles's Funeral Oration, while admittedly not a direct quotation from the historical figure, attempts to report what was said at the time and gives a true window into the values not only of Pericles himself but also of the Athenian democracy he was praising in the oration.

From a close reading perspective, whether the study occurs in an English or a social studies class, the complete speech is too long to be close read in its entirety. For that reason, choosing the proper close reading passage presents our first challenge in planning for studying this text. The entire oration is too long to reprint here but is widely available online. In selecting a passage for close reading, we should keep in mind the general rule: the passage should fit comfortably on a single side of an 8.5 × 11–inch page. At the same time, the passage must be useful in developing students' understanding for the focus of the lesson. So, trying to limit our selection to a single page of text, let's consider the various ways teachers might teach this passage.

In the most general terms, the oration is divided into two sections. The occasion is the burial of fallen Athenian soldiers early in the war, which eventually leads to the downfall of Athens. The first section focuses on what makes Athenian society so different from other Greek city-states. The latter portion turns to consideration of the dead, but within the context of a celebration of Athens.

In a social studies class, this text allows students to explore the elements of Athenian democracy at the time. For students to identify the values Pericles proclaims and consider whether these values are substantially different than those of modern democracies would likely be among the goals of a close reading of the Funeral Oration. For this reason, we might choose one to two paragraphs that specifically address some of those values. One possibility would be paragraphs six through eight, in which Pericles describes the specifics of Athenian democracy. Another possibility would be paragraph ten (beginning "Our love of what is beautiful . . ."; as cited in Finley, 1972, p. 147), which specifically describes the values of Athenians and the democratic ways individual citizens interact with each other. Teachers could use both selections to accomplish the goal of examining the values of Athenian democracy.

Another approach, perhaps appropriate for an English class, is to see this text as a persuasive speech. In this context, we might explore Pericles's perceived purpose in giving the speech and then focus more narrowly on his methods of rhetoric—the way in which he goes about convincing his audience of his argument. If we are considering the oration as a persuasive speech and want to look at Pericles's rhetorical process, paragraph fourteen (beginning "So and such they were, these men . . ."; as cited in Finley, 1972, p. 149) lends itself well. In this section, Pericles has turned his attention to the dead soldiers, describing them as heroes and attempting to connect his praise of them with his earlier praise of Athenian democracy. It has strong rhetorical elements and lends itself well to rhetorical analysis. That excerpt is:

> So and such they were, these men—worthy of their city. We who remain behind may hope to be spared their fate, but must resolve to keep the same daring spirit against the foe. It is not simply a question of estimating the advantages in theory. I could tell you a long story (and you know it as well as I do) about what is to be gained by beating the enemy back. What I would prefer is that you should fix your eyes every day on the greatness of Athens as she really is, and should fall in love with her. When you realize her greatness, then reflect that what made her great was men with a spirit of adventure, men who knew their duty, men who were ashamed to fall below a certain standard. If they ever failed in an enterprise, they made up their minds that at any rate the city should not find their courage lacking to her, and they gave to her the best contribution that they could.

> They gave her their lives, to her and to all of us, and for their own selves they won praises that never grow old, the most splendid of sepulchers—not the sepulcher in which their bodies are laid, but where their glory remains eternal in men's minds, always there on the right occasion to stir others to speech or to action. For famous men have the whole earth as their memorial. It is not only the inscriptions on their graves in their own country that mark them out; no, in foreign lands also, not in any visible form but in people's hearts, their memory abides and grows. It is for you to try to be like them. Make up your minds that happiness depends on being free, and freedom depends on being courageous. Let there be no relaxation in fact of the perils of the war.

> The people who have most excuse for despising death are not the wretched and unfortunate, who have no hope of doing well for themselves, but those who run the risk of a complete reversal in

their lives, and who would feel the difference most intensely if things went wrong for them. Any intelligent man would find a humiliation caused by his own slackness more painful to bear than death, when death comes to him unperceived, in battle, and in the confidence of his patriotism. (as cited in Finley, 1972, pp. 149–150)

This excerpt will serve as the basis for our example.

Prereading

This text is a funeral speech, and there are multiple ways to access the idea of praising those who have died. Importantly, these soldiers died for a very public cause, so if we are to access students' prior knowledge, we would want to have them think about public events rather than the passing of a relative or friend. This is both more relevant to this text and emotionally safer for students. A simple journal entry about their own attitudes toward soldiers who have died in the service of their country will likely engage students in the process quickly. We might also ask students to briefly discuss a modern equivalent of the Funeral Oration, such as a world leader's remarks following a loss of life in his or her country. One obvious word of caution though is about those students who may have experienced personal loss in this area. For these students, such memories may be far too painful. If this is a concern, teachers may wish to approach the prereading of this text from a completely different angle.

The other purpose of the Funeral Oration is a praise of Athenian democracy. From this perspective, accessing students' background knowledge could involve asking them to think about democratic values in the United States. Discussion questions might include the following.

- "Is America a democracy?"

- "Does American democracy apply to all citizens equally?"

- "Is American democracy the best system of government in the world?"

- "Should America promote democracy in other countries?"

Each of these questions can be a valuable way to examine what students know and their opinions about democracy.

Depending on the close reading focus for this text, it may be appropriate to have students read the entire text before focusing on a short passage for close reading. This could be done as an in-class silent reading or as a homework assignment. There are situations where the larger document could distract students from the focus of the excerpt, but in the case of our excerpt, the larger context supports the close reading passage.

Reading Twice and Annotating

Having engaged in prereading and having worked their way through the close reading passage at least once, it is time to introduce our close reading passage. After a student has read the excerpt twice and annotated, figure B.7 (page 134) depicts what might appear.

Note that the annotations in figure B.7 reveal an understanding on two levels—one aimed at meaning and another dealing with rhetorical devices. Eventually, these two factors will merge in the student's understanding, but it is unlikely this will happen in the first couple of readings. As we now turn to a discussion of what students have found in the passage, we will want to provide opportunities for students to share their evidence and ideas in both areas.

An appeal to patriotism →

So and such they were these men—worthy of their city. We who remain behind may hope to be spared their fate, but must resolve to keep the same daring spirit against the foe. It is not simply a question of estimating the advantages in theory. I could tell you a long story (and you know it as well as I do) about what is to be gained by beating the enemy back. What I would prefer is that you should fix your eyes every day on the greatness of Athens as she really is, and should fall in love with her. When you realize her greatness, then reflect that what made her great was men with a spirit of adventure, men who knew their duty, men who were ashamed to fall below a certain standard. If they ever failed in an enterprise, they made up their minds that at any rate the city should not find their courage lacking to her, and they gave to her the best contribution that they could.

This is surprising in an oration about fallen soldiers. He is deflecting the attention away from the soldiers and to Athens. Why?

Here's the connection for the question above. All of these descriptions appeal to emotions →

Placing Athens above themselves. So they are good examples to everyone else.

Complicated sentence, and it places value on fame beyond human life's value. Would this have surprised his audience? →

They gave her their lives, to her and to all of us, and for their own selves they won praises that never grow old, the most splendid of sepulchers—not the sepulcher in which their bodies are laid, but where their glory remains eternal in men's minds, always there on the right occasion to stir others to speech or to action. For famous men have the whole earth as their memorial. It is not only the inscriptions on their graves in their own country that mark them out; no, in foreign lands also, not in any visible form but in people's hearts, their memory abides and grows. It is for you to try to be like them. Make up your minds that happiness depends on being free, and freedom depends on being courageous. Let there be no relaxation in fact of the perils of the war.

An emotional appeal →

Short sentence after many long ones.

The people who have most excuse for despising death are not the wretched and unfortunate, who have no hope of doing well for themselves, but those who run the risk of a complete reversal in their lives, and who would feel the difference most intensely if things went wrong for them. Any intelligent man would find a humiliation caused by his own slackness more painful to bear than death, when death comes to him unperceived, in battle, and in the confidence of his patriotism.

Is this really true? Would Athenians agree?

Source: Finley, 1972, pp. 149–150.

Figure B.7: Reading and annotating Pericles's Funeral Oration.

Generating Questions

The focus of our lesson is on the rhetorical effect of the speech, and in this particular close reading passage, we will at some point want to focus on the rhetorical methods. That will determine the kind of discussion as we attempt to guide students to generate a specific analytical reading question for their return to the passage. However, it is best to begin by seeing what is in students' minds after they wrestle with the passage a couple of times.

Often, students want to jump immediately to meaning or theme and their own opinions about these issues. In an initial discussion to generate questions, focusing on theme and meaning is fine as long as we rather quickly ask students to back up their opinions with evidence from the text. Analytical questions for this passage may apply to both overall meaning and rhetorical method. The following questions are possibilities that reflect the way most tenth-grade students react to the passage.

1. Why would Pericles focus more on Athens than on the dead soldiers?

2. Which of the three rhetorical appeals—logos, ethos, or pathos—is the primary method in this passage, and why?

The second question will focus students on the rhetorical methods of the text, and since that is the focus of our lesson, it is the one we should direct students to attack as we proceed to the fourth step of the close reading process. (For more information about the three rhetorical appeals, see chapter 3, page 41.) Eventually, the class will answer the first question, but that will come later, after a thorough analysis of the passage, and, perhaps, after seeing the passage in the larger context of the entire oration.

When we ask students to return to the passage for a close analytical reading of the text, we want them to identify evidence that supports an argument about the primary form of rhetorical appeal in this passage. They may easily see the correct choice of the three appeals; they may have a much harder time supporting that choice with direct text evidence.

Reading Analytically

With the focus question (Which of the three rhetorical appeals—logos, ethos, or pathos—is the primary method in this passage, and why?) in front of them, we can ask students to do a careful and detailed analytical close reading of the passage. Figure B.8 (page 136) shows how a student might add to the original comments on the passage. In reality, these additional annotations could very well be made on the same paper as the first round of annotations. For clarity, however, figure B.8 depicts only the new notes.

Once again, the student has dug deeper into the mechanics of the passage, and clearly can make an argument for the correct answer—this is an appeal of pathos argument. In the discussion phase, the class will explore exactly how that occurs.

Discussing as a Class

We must keep in mind the following two focus questions the class developed prior to the analytical reading stage.

1. Why would Pericles focus more on Athens than on the dead soldiers?

2. Which of the three rhetorical appeals—logos, ethos, or pathos—is the primary method in this passage, and why?

"Daring spirit" is emotional too—talking about courage.

Here Pericles is moving away from logic, so this moves away from a logos appeal. If you're doing more than "estimating the advantages" you're doing more than logic.

Back to talking about courage—emotional appeal

Fame is not a logical appeal; it is emotional.

Really? I guess if you're attempting to make people like the men because of their deeds, this makes sense.

Back to courage again

So and such they were these men—worthy of their city. We who remain behind may hope to be spared their fate, but must resolve to keep the same daring spirit against the foe. It is not simply a question of estimating the advantages in theory. I could tell you a long story (and you know it as well as I do) about what is to be gained by beating the enemy back. What I would prefer is that you should fix your eyes every day on the greatness of Athens as she really is, and should fall in love with her. When you realize her greatness, then reflect that what made her great was men with a spirit of adventure, men who knew their duty, men who were ashamed to fall below a certain standard. If they ever failed in an enterprise, they made up their minds that at any rate the city should not find their courage lacking to her, and they gave to her the best contribution that they could.

They gave her their lives, to her and to all of us, and for their own selves they won praises that never grow old, the most splendid of sepulchers—not the sepulcher in which their bodies are laid, but where their glory remains eternal in men's minds, always there on the right occasion to stir others to speech or to action. For famous men have the whole earth as their memorial. It is not only the inscriptions on their graves in their own country that mark them out; no, in foreign lands also, not in any visible form but in people's hearts, their memory abides and grows. It is for you to try to be like them. Make up your minds that happiness depends on being free, and freedom depends on being courageous. Let there be no relaxation in fact of the perils of the war.

The people who have most excuse for despising death are not the wretched and unfortunate, who have no hope of doing well for themselves, but those who run the risk of a complete reversal in their lives, and who would feel the difference most intensely if things went wrong for them. Any intelligent man would find a humiliation caused by his own slackness more painful to bear than death, when death comes to him unperceived, in battle, and in the confidence of his patriotism.

This word has a strong emotional appeal. If we think someone is worthy, we are judging him based on values. And values connect with our emotions.

Pericles would rather his listeners focus on the "greatness of Athens." That appeals to patriotism, and that is emotional.

Refers to Athens as female. Probably tradition, but also emotional—men (citizens) love women.

This is basically not logical—you run a risk of losing everything. Emotionally you would do that; logically you wouldn't.

Not sure what this means . . .

- The basic appeal here is pathos. There is a lot of evidence of emotional appeal.
- Why use pathos appeal? The situation is a funeral, where people will be somewhat emotional. So the audience is primed for that kind of appeal.
- Pericles knows that the most powerful way to honor the dead will be emotional.

Source: Finley, 1972, pp. 149–150.

Figure B.8: Analytical reading of Pericles's Funeral Oration.

Although the second question has been the direct focus of the students' reading, it should be the initial and major focus of the discussion. The first question will make a good ending to the discussion since the answer to it lies in the answer to the second question. The following narrative with commentary, figure B.9, is how the discussion might proceed.

Narrative	Commentary
Teacher: We've taken the time for a careful reading of the passage, and with a direct focus on the question, Which of the three rhetorical appeals—logos, ethos, or pathos—is the primary method in this passage, and why? I'm going to ask you to choose one of the three appeals you feel is the major focus and then support that choice with some evidence from the text. Remember, our purpose here is to be grounded solidly in what the text says, so that, for example, if you were asked to analyze this passage on a state test you could easily write a strong essay with good support. Anyone wish to start?	Teacher sets the mission for the discussion, reminding students not only of their immediate task but also of the relevancy of the entire close reading process.
Student 1: My vote is for a pathos appeal. It seems to me that he uses a lot of emotionally loaded words here—words like *worthy* and *spirit*.	Right away we have the correct answer.
Teacher: Anyone else wish to jump on the pathos bandwagon?	Allows many others to get in on being correct.
Student 2: Yeah, I think there's a lot of evidence for it. I mean, look at the verbs in the second sentence—*hope* and *resolve*. They are strong words, but they have a very powerful emotional appeal too.	Now students begin to give evidence, and it is pretty solid evidence.
Student 3: And there are other words that do that, like "greatness of Athens" and "fall in love with her."	
Student 4: I thought about that pronoun, *her*. I don't think of my city as female, but apparently they did. If you're thinking of a city as a person you could fall in love with the city. Definitely an emotional appeal.	This is a remarkable observation for a tenth grader. The pronoun use is subtle but effective.
Teacher: Does anyone wish to make an argument for logos or ethos? (No response)	Before we go too far down the pathos path, we have to give the opportunity for other answers, or students will feel intimidated about offering answers that disagree with the majority of the class discussion. Fortunately, no one disagrees, so we can proceed with the evidence.
Teacher: OK, we have lots of diction evidence. Do we have any other kind of evidence?	We've dealt with the easy stuff. How about the hard stuff?
Student 5: I found an image that supports emotion. In the middle of the passage he says, "For famous men have the whole earth as their memorial." At first I didn't understand what he was saying there. But after I thought about it a while, I think he's saying that if you get famous because you did this great heroic deed, all the world will know about it and remember it. And if you think about the audience there in Athens, thinking about these dead soldiers, it is right at that point that their fame is starting, and it could spread across the whole world, and people would think that is great and be very emotional about it.	This is a fine example and, although the student's explanation isn't very sophisticated, she has the right idea about how the image is working.

Figure B.9: A sample narrative with commentary for Pericles's Funeral Oration.

continued →

Narrative	Commentary
Teacher: Anyone else focus on that image? Want to say more? (No response)	Sometimes when someone takes the discussion in a new direction, students need a moment to focus on it and think. No immediate response.
Teacher: There's actually a bit more to that image.	A hint.
Student 2: I thought about the sentences that follow the one we were just talking about. It says, "It is not only the inscriptions on their graves in their own country that mark them out; no, in foreign lands also, not in any visible form but in people's hearts, their memory abides and grows." I thought that was really powerful, because it talks about the way people think about these guys in their hearts, and that is their emotions.	Student 2 takes the bait. Here, the teacher has made it OK to talk about more than the single portion of the sentence that student 5 discussed.
Student 6: There's also some more to it before the line about the "whole earth." There is imagery in the line about sepulchers. I looked it up and it means vaults for burial. So when Pericles says "the most splendid of sepulchers—not the sepulcher in which their bodies are laid, but where their glory remains eternal in men's minds," he is talking about something emotional—memories people have.	Student 6 takes the evidence to an even broader level, and he is right—the image is substantially larger than has been discussed so far. Good job!
Teacher: OK, we've had diction and imagery on the table. Is there anything else we need to discuss? Other techniques. (No response)	We've got good evidence, but can we go further.
Teacher: If we have diction and if we have imagery, we have two elements of what?	Leading the discussion—sometimes they need to see the right question to ask for the next step.
Student 4: Tone.	Correct answer.
Teacher: Right! So, how about that most difficult of questions, "What is the tone of the passage?" (No response)	Teacher phrases it to be less threatening—admits this is a tough question. Tone is the hardest rhetorical device for students to get correct. That's why there is no immediate response. Some students probably have ideas about it, but it is too threatening to try and be wrong.
Teacher: Tone is made up of diction, imagery, language, details, and syntax. We've got two of those elements on the table already, diction and imagery. So we can make a guess at the answer, even if we haven't been able to look at any of the other factors. So, given what we've said about diction and imagery, what would be a guess about the tone of the passage?	A reminder of lessons already taught. The teacher is directing students to do some induction—given the evidence, can you bring it together to draw a conclusion? And the teacher couches it in the right term—*guess*. Anybody can guess and be wrong. Give it a try.
Student 5: I'd say praise. He's saying a lot of emotional things about these soldiers, praising them, and wanting people to remember them.	Not a bad first try.

Teacher: OK, we have one vote for praise. Any other thoughts? (None)	They're still not sure, and praise sounded pretty good.
Teacher: Remember what we said about tone. The right answer for tone is at the center of the target, but we can't get to the center just yet because we don't have enough evidence. Just get on the target. Any other ideas?	Reminder that the standard here isn't precision at the moment—just get some ideas out there we can discuss.
Student 7: I would say it is more like honorable—he's honoring their memory by putting it together with people's emotions about their country and saying the men will be remembered by the world for being heroes.	This is pretty close to the right answer. And it is good enough given the evidence we have right now.
Teacher: What do you think? (About half the class thinks that's a good answer.)	Asking for response—general agreement.
Teacher: I think praise is a part of honoring someone, but honorable might be a better choice for a tone, at least at this stage. OK, good job. Where does our discussion go next?	Important to acknowledge the first offering (because if you don't there will be fewer and fewer first offerings), but nail down honorable as the current right answer. Now turn the discussion back to the students. They need to know where to go next. The right answer is to attempt to answer the two focus questions thoroughly.
Student 8: I think we've answered the first focus question.	Oops.
Student 5: Not really. We answered which was the primary appeal, but did we get to why?	Correct!
Teacher: OK, can we focus on that part for a moment? Why does Pericles choose to use a pathos appeal? (Little response)	Officially stating the task.
Teacher: Let's turn to the person sitting next to you and have a two-minute discussion on why Pericles would use a pathos appeal. (Two minutes of discussion)	When the task is tough, there is safety in numbers. Have them test their ideas where it has much less impact if they are wrong.
Teacher: OK, back to our class discussion. Why does Pericles choose a pathos appeal?	Re-establishing the task.
Student 3: If the purpose is to honor the dead heroes, what better way to honor them than to get people emotional over what they did? And it makes sense to have people thinking about their sacrifice in terms of the war that Athens is fighting and get people emotionally behind the war again.	We get to the right answer here, and it is relatively easy given the close reading that has been done.
Student 1: That's what we were saying too. It's very patriotic, and that is what you want in the middle of the war. People will be more patriotic if you bring out their emotions about the war.	Further support. Good job!

continued →

Narrative	Commentary
Teacher: Anyone else want to add to that? (No response)	Offering the chance to get in on being correct.
Teacher: Sounds like a good answer to me, and we could turn around and claim that answer as the why and support it with the evidence we cited before as the how, couldn't we? (General agreement)	Important to place the work in a larger context—the kind of task they might be asked on an assessment.
Teacher: Well, that leaves just one question, the first focus question, "Why would Pericles focus more on Athens than on the dead soldiers?" Please turn to those sitting near you and discuss that question. I'll write it on the board. Now that we understand the passage more deeply, how would we answer that question? (Time to discuss)	Teacher now turns to the first question. Because the answer doesn't immediately follow from the current discussion, students need time to process the answer.
Teacher: OK, you've had time to talk. How would you answer the question on the board?	Brings them back.
Student 5: Well, I'm not sure he does focus on Athens more than the soldiers. After our reading, I think I'd say that the focus stays on the soldiers most of the time.	Now the answer is clear. Sometimes it takes a close reading to realize that the question wasn't quite correct at the start. Nothing wrong with that, as long as we establish it by the end of the discussion.
Student 2: Yes, but he does talk about Athens, and I think it is to make people patriotic about the war and to honor the soldiers by connecting them with their patriotic duty in the war. **Teacher:** Agree? Disagree? Qualify? (No comments) **Teacher:** Good job! I agree.	

Using Processing Activities

The final step in our close reading analysis is to examine the class's conclusions about the passage in a broader sense as part of a processing activity. Pericles's Funeral Oration offers a wide variety of opportunities for taking the evidence to the next level. One is to consider the excerpt in light of the entire work. In this case, we can now ask students to read the entire oration again, with an eye toward the conclusions they have already drawn about the focus on Athens in a patriotic sense as the background for developing an emotional appreciation in his audience for the deeds of the dead soldiers. As students encounter the entire work again, they will find resonances throughout the speech of these very conclusions, and they will also notice that Pericles's (and thus Thucydides's) rhetorical choices are all of one pattern, one method—to raise an emotional reaction in an audience in need of a patriotic renewal as their long war continues.

Another traditional activity is to compare this speech to other funeral orations, and teachers often use Abraham Lincoln's Gettysburg Address. Students will find many parallels and some differences between that famous speech and Pericles's text from two thousand years earlier. A deeper processing opportunity builds from such a comparison. If we can compare the rhetorical choices of two political leaders, the texts offer the opportunity for comparing more than just the speeches. Students could consider questions like the following.

- In what ways do the speeches' represented democracies compare?

- Is Athenian democracy the true precursor of American democracy in the 19th century?

- Can we understand shared and different values from the two speeches, and can those values be the basis of a broader comparison of the societies?

Such a comparison, whether it takes the form of a written analysis, an oral presentation, or a debate, would require further student research.

Another processing activity option is a performance task. A funeral oration, by its very nature, provides a fine opportunity for interpretive speeches. Students (in character) present the particular close reading passage or several passages from the oration. When students prepare to read the speech aloud, the work they have done to understand Pericles's rhetorical choices serves as the basis for their reading. An assignment of this type requires some instruction about how to translate analysis of the written word into the spoken word, but the result may be some very meaningful and entertaining public speeches. Students may feel less intimidated about speaking in front of their peers after they have deeply analyzed and understood the passage they are presenting.

Finally, the persuasive essay is always an effective processing activity. Once students have carefully read the passage, gathered evidence, and drawn conclusions, they will have the basis of a strong persuasive essay. The structure of that essay will be fairly easy to develop, and teachers can focus on any number of aspects of a strong persuasive piece, be it a well-developed introduction, a strong conclusion, or strongly developed support paragraphs focusing on textual evidence.

REFERENCES AND RESOURCES

ACT. (2006). *Reading between the lines: What the ACT reveals about college readiness in reading.* Iowa City, IA: Author.

Aristotle. (350 BCE). *Rhetoric.* (W. R. Roberts, Trans.). Accessed at http://classics.mit.edu/Aristo=le /rhetoric.html on July 28, 2017.

Aristotle. (1997). *Poetics.* (S. H. Butcher, Trans.). Mineola, NY: Dover. (Original work published 335 BCE).

Arp, T. R., & Johnson, G. (2009). *Perrine's literature: Structure, sound, and sense* (10th ed.). Boston, MA: Wadsworth Cengage Learning.

Austen, J. (1995). *Pride and prejudice.* Mineola, NY: Dover. (Original work published 1813).

Bauer, S. W. (2003). *The well-educated mind: A guide to the classical education you never had.* New York: Norton.

Booth, W. C. (1961). *The rhetoric of fiction.* Chicago: University of Chicago Press.

Burns, R. (1794). "A red, red rose." Accessed at https://poetryfoundation.org/poems/43812/a-red-red -rose on July 28, 2017.

Chopin, K. (1994). *The Awakening: An authoritative text, biographical and historical contexts, criticism.* (M. Culley, Ed.). New York: Norton. (Original work published 1899).

Common Core State Standards Initiative. (n.d.). *Key shifts in English language arts.* Accessed at www .corestandards.org/other-resources/key-shifts-in-english-language-arts on May 13, 2017.

Crews, F. C. (n.d.). *Literary criticism.* Accessed at https://britannica.com/topic/literary-criticism/The -20th-century on May 6, 2017.

Culture Shock. (n.d.). Huck Finn *in context: A teaching guide.* Accessed at https://pbs.org/wgbh /cultureshock/teachers/huck/index.html on July 28, 2017.

Dickens, C. (1977). *Bleak house.* (G. Ford & S. Monod, Eds.). New York: Norton. (Original work published 1853).

Dweck, C. S. (2006). *Mindset: The new psychology of success.* New York: Ballantine Books.

Eliot, G. (1856). The natural history of German life. *Westminster Review, 66.* Accessed at https://bl.uk /collection-items/the-natural-history-of-german-life-essay-by-george-eliot-from-the-westminster-review# on May 6, 2017.

Ericsson, K. A., Krampe, R. T., & Tesch-Römer, C. (1993). The role of deliberate practice in the acquisition of expert performance. *Psychological Review, 100*(3), 363–406.

Evans, G. B., & Tobin, J. J. M. (Eds.). (1997). *The riverside Shakespeare* (2nd ed.). Boston: Houghton Mifflin.

Finley, M. I. (Ed.). (1972). *Thucydides: History of the Peloponnesian war.* (R. Warner, Trans.). Harmondsworth, United Kingdom: Penguin Books.

Frank, A. (1997). *The diary of a young girl.* (O. H. Frank & M. Pressler, Eds.; S. Massotty, Trans.). New York: Bantam. (Original work published 1947).

Freytag, G. (1876). *Die technik des dramas.* Accessed at https://archive.org/details/dietechnikdesdra 00frey on May 8, 2017.

Goff, D. A., Pratt, C., & Ong, B. (2005). The relations between children's reading comprehension, working memory, language skills and components of reading decoding in a normal sample. *Reading and Writing, 18*(7–9), 583–616.

Great Books Foundation. (Ed.). (1990). *Introduction to great books, first series, leader's guide.* Chicago: Author.

Harmon, W., & Holman, C. H. (2003). *A handbook to literature* (9th ed.). Upper Saddle River, NJ: Prentice Hall.

Hart, B., & Risley, T. R. (1995). *Meaningful differences in the everyday experience of young American children.* Baltimore: Brookes.

Hart, B., & Risley, T. R. (2003). The early catastrophe: The 30 million word gap by age 3. *American Educator, 27*(1), 4–9.

Historical criticism. (2014). In *Encyclopedia Britannica.* Accessed at https://britannica.com/topic/historical-criticism-literary-criticism on May 6, 2017.

Johnson, S. (1781). *The lives of the most eminent English poets.* Accessed at https://archive.org/details /livesmosteminen33johngoog on May 6, 2017.

Kamil, M. L., & Hiebert, E. H. (2005). Teaching and learning vocabulary: Perspectives and persistent issues. In E. H. Hiebert & M. L. Kamil (Eds.), *Teaching and learning vocabulary: Bringing research to practice* (pp. 1–23). Mahwah, NJ: Erlbaum.

Kendall, J. S. (2011). *Understanding Common Core State Standards.* Alexandria, VA: Association for Supervision and Curriculum Development.

Kiszla, M. (2017, May 6). Slumping Rockies shortstop Trevor Story might need trip to minors to fix holes in his swing. *The Denver Post.* Accessed at www.denverpost.com/2017/05/06/trevor-story-slump -minors-fix-swing on May 7, 2017.

Lunsford, A. A., Ruszkiewicz, J. J., & Walters, K. (2004). *Everything's an argument: With readings* (3rd ed.). Boston: Bedford/St. Martin's.

Magee, B. (2001). *The story of philosophy.* New York: Dorling Kindersley.

Marzano Research. (2016a). Engaging students in cognitively complex tasks [Folio]. *The Marzano Compendium of Instructional Strategies.* Accessed at www.marzanoresearch.com/online-compendium on April 10, 2017.

Marzano Research. (2016b). Previewing [Folio]. *The Marzano Compendium of Instructional Strategies.* Accessed at www.marzanoresearch.com/online-compendium on April 10, 2017.

Marzano Research. (2016c). Understanding students' backgrounds and interests [Folio]. *The Marzano Compendium of Instructional Strategies*. Accessed at www.marzanoresearch.com/online-compendium on April 10, 2017.

Marzano, R. J. (with Marzano, J. S., & Pickering, D. J.). (2003). *Classroom management that works: Research-based strategies for every teacher*. Alexandria, VA: Association for Supervision and Curriculum Development.

Marzano, R. J. (2010). *Formative assessment & standards-based grading*. Bloomington, IN: Marzano Research.

Marzano, R. J. (2017). *The new art and science of teaching*. Bloomington, IN: Solution Tree Press.

Marzano, R. J., Frontier, T., & Livingston, D. (2011). *Effective supervision: Supporting the art and science of teaching*. Alexandria, VA: Association for Supervision and Curriculum Development.

Marzano, R. J., Norford, J. S., Finn, M., & Finn, D., III (with Mestaz, R., & Selleck, R.). (2017). *A handbook for personalized competency-based education*. Bloomington, IN: Marzano Research.

Marzano, R. J., Pickering, D. J., & Pollock, J. E. (2001). *Classroom instruction that works: Research-based strategies for increasing student achievement*. Alexandria, VA: Association for Supervision and Curriculum Development.

Marzano, R. J., Pickering, D., & Pollock, J. E. (2005). *Classroom instruction that works: Research-based strategies for increasing student achievement*. Upper Saddle River, NJ: Prentice Hall.

Marzano, R. J., Scott, D., Boogren, T. H., & Newcomb, M. L. (2017). *Motivating & inspiring students: Strategies to awaken the learner*. Bloomington, IN: Marzano Research.

McKeown, M. G., Beck, I. L., & Blake, R. G. (2009). Rethinking reading comprehension instruction: A comparison of instruction for strategies and content approaches. *Reading Research Quarterly, 44*(3), 218–253.

Miller, A. (2009). Death of a salesman. In T. R. Arp & G. Johnson (Eds.), *Perrine's literature: Structure, sound, and sense* (pp. 1449–1530). Boston: Wadsworth Cengage Learning. (Original work published 1949).

Montag, W. (1992). The "workshop of filthy creation": A Marxist reading of *Frankenstein*. In M. W. Shelley, *Frankenstein* (J. M. Smith, Ed.) (pp. 300–311). Boston: St. Martin's.

National Governors Association Center for Best Practices & Council of Chief State School Officers. (2010). *Common Core State Standards for English language arts & literacy in history/social studies, science, and technical subjects*. Washington, DC: Authors.

National Reading Panel. (2000). *Teaching children to read: An evidence-based assessment of the scientific research literature on reading and its implications for reading instruction*. Washington, DC: National Institutes of Health.

Nelson, J., Perfetti, C., Liben, D., & Liben, M. (2012). *Measures of text difficulty: Testing their predictive value for grade levels and student performance*. Washington, DC: Council of Chief State Officers.

Paige, D. D. (2011). Engaging struggling adolescent readers through situational interest: A model proposing the relationships among extrinsic motivation, oral reading fluency, comprehension, and academic achievement. *Reading Psychology, 32*(5), 395–425.

Pearson, P. D., & Liben, D. (2013). *The progression of reading comprehension*. Accessed at http://achievethecore.org/page/1195/the-progression-of-reading-comprehension on May 13, 2017.

Plato. (1992). *The republic*. (A. D. Lindsay, Trans.). New York: Knopf. (Original work published 380 BCE).

Popkin, R. H. (2000). *The Columbia history of Western philosophy*. New York: Columbia University Press.

Richter, D. H. (2007). *The critical tradition: Classic texts and contemporary trends*. Boston: Bedford/St. Martin's.

Richter, D. H. (Ed.). (1998). *The critical tradition: Classic texts and contemporary trends* (2nd ed.). Boston: Bedford Books.

Rogers, K., & Simms, J. A. (2015). *Teaching argumentation: Activities and games for the classroom*. Bloomington, IN: Marzano Research.

Sandburg, C. (1916). "Fog." Accessed at www.poetryfoundation.org/poems-and-poets/poems/detail/45032 on April 15, 2017.

Scott, A., & Newbold, C. (2017, May 30). *DIDLS strategy for analyzing tone*. Accessed at http://thevisualcommunicationguy.com/2017/04/18/didls-strategy-for-analyzing-tone on January 5, 2018.

Shakespeare, W. (1997a). *As you like it*. In G. B. Evans & J. M. M. Tobin (Eds.), *The riverside Shakespeare: The complete works* (2nd ed.). Boston: Houghton Mifflin. (Original work published 1623).

Shakespeare, W. (1997b). *Romeo and Juliet*. In G. B. Evans & J. M. M. Tobin (Eds.), *The riverside Shakespeare: The complete works* (2nd ed.). Boston: Houghton Mifflin. (Original work published 1595).

Shelley, M. W. (1992). *Frankenstein: Complete, authoritative text with biographical and historical contexts, critical history, and essays from five contemporary critical perspectives* (J. M. Smith, Ed.). Boston: Bedford/St. Martin's. (Original work published 1818).

Stanovich, K. E. (1986). Matthew effects in reading: Some consequences of individual differences in the acquisition of literacy. *Reading Research Quarterly, 21*(4), 360–407.

Student Achievement Partners. (2016). *Research supporting the ELA standards and shifts*. Accessed at http://achievethecore.org/page/2669/research-supporting-the-ela-standards-and-shifts on May 13, 2017.

Swift, J. (1996). *A modest proposal and other satitical works*. New York: Dover. (Original work published 1729).

Thucydides, & Finley, M. I. (Ed.). (1972). *The history of the Peloponnesian war* (R. Warner, Trans.). Baltimore: Penguin Books. (Original work published 431–405 BCE).

Tolkien, J. R. R. (1974). *The hobbit: Or there and back again*. New York: Ballantine Books.

Twain, M. (1999). *The Adventures of Huckleberry Finn: An authoritative context and sources, criticism* (T. Cooley, Ed.). New York: Norton. (Original work published 1884).

United States. (1776). *The Declaration of Independence: A transcription*. The U.S. National Archives and Records Administration. Accessed at https://archives.gov/founding-docs/declaration-transcript on May 10, 2017.

Wharton, E. (1992). *Ethan Frome*. New York: Signet Classics. (Original work published 1911).

Whitman, W. (1991). *Leaves of grass*. New York: Oxford University Press. (Original work published 1855).

Woolf, V., & Gordon, M. (2005). *A room of one's own*. Orlando: Harcourt. (Original work published in 1929).

Woolf, V. (1989). *To the lighthouse*. New York: Harcourt. (Original work published 1927).

Wordsworth, W. (1992). *Favorite poems*. New York: Dover Publications.

INDEX

MARZANO Research

Ensure all students achieve academic success

 Signature PD Service

The New Art & Science of Teaching Workshop

The New Art and Science of Teaching is a well-researched instructional framework that comprehensively addresses the most alterable effect on student achievement—quality instruction. One of the major changes in The New Art and Science of Teaching is the focus on student outcomes obtained by teachers' instructional actions. The premise is that teachers who implement instructional strategies will, in turn, help students use mental processes that successively enhance the learning. In other words, it's not enough to merely use an instructional strategy, but more important to ensure it has the desired learning effect for students.

- Gain an awareness of the research related to the elements of The New Art & Science of Teaching.
- Learn the instructional framework components, which include: 3 categories, 10 design questions, and 43 elements.
- Experience many of the 43 elements through hundreds of modeled instructional strategies.
- Use reflective guides as a means of enhancing instructional practices.

- Explore how the companion online compendium can support the model by highlighting 300 instructional strategies, video descriptions, and print resources related to the new design questions and all 43 elements.
- Examine how eight systems changes support the implementation of The New Art & Science of Teaching.

Learn more
MarzanoResearch.com/NASOTPD